BRANDED
FOR
GOD

Jim Durbin

Cowboy Chaplin

ACKNOWLEDGEMENTS

As I am not a very good typist or computer whiz, I wrote this book in long hand. I want to thank the following for their help in making this book possible:

To God, my heavenly Father, who without his prodding and inspiration I would not have written this book.

My daughter, Kristin Hanson, and my wife, Judy, for their many hours of research, typing and help editing this book.

My step-son, Sean Smith, and my barrel racing students, Madison and Ava Syres, for their pencil illustrations that appear before each chapter.

My step-daughter, Stefanie Miller, for her formatting of the pencil illustrations .

Paula Scott Bicknell and James Burgess, both gifted writers in their own right, for reading my book, their words of encouragement and for their helpful suggestions to make this book a better read.

My children, their spouses, my grandchildren, my entire family and friends who have listened to me through all the time I talked about writing this book and yet have encouraged and supported me in the writing of it.

CONTENTS

INTRODUCTION

I am writing this book to share with others what I have learned from God's word about life's struggles and to share my spiritual journey of faith. I lived my life on the wide way my first twenty-six years. Because of God's grace and mercy, I decided to change my address to the narrow way of life and not my way.

Through my own struggles in life I have personally needed healing, mercy, forgiveness and His presence in times of loneliness. I have experienced mild PTSD, depression, fear and worry. I saw a lot of heartache and many unpleasant events during my years in law enforcement. I have learned God is always faithful and if we will humble ourselves before Him, He will meet us and provide comfort for our thirsty soul. Over the years since I have accepted Jesus as my Savior, I have hidden God's word in my heart. God has used me as I draw from my own experiences and share God's word to counsel, advise and inspire others who are experiencing problems.

My dreams while growing up were to be a sheriff deputy and a cowboy. I have been blessed to be both and it is from many of my own experiences and knowledge of God's word that I share in order to help others. My adventurous life has been filled with excitement and joy serving the Lord, my community, family and friends.

This book is by a common man in simple language for easy reading. Within this book I share some personal testimonies of God's grace in my life. I am not a perfect man and if you follow me around all day you would confirm my assessment. However, I am dedicated to building a productive relationship that pleases God.

My purpose for writing this book is to direct people to Jesus Christ, our Lord and Savior. He has been my friend, counselor and protector in my cowboy and law enforcement careers.

My prayer is you will be encouraged, strengthened in your faith and will invest more time with God and His word. Don't be afraid to lean on Him in times of trouble. After all He loves you and gave His life for you. I pray the contents of this book will give you hope, comfort and be spiritually beneficial in your life. May your trails be bright and your load be light. God bless you.

John 12:32 *"And I, if I be lifted up from the earth, will draw all men unto me." (KJV)*

1
CHILDHOOD
MEMORIES

Luke 18:16-17 *"Permit the children to come to Me, and do not hinder them, for the kingdom of God belongs to such as these. 17 Truly I say to you, whoever does*

4

*not receive the kingdom of God like a child
will not enter it at all."*

On a hallway wall we have photos of our family. One of these is an old black and white photo of my mom, dad, brother and me. My brother, Al, was nine years old and I was twelve years old. Mom and dad were sitting on chairs under a tree; Al was standing beside mom; and I was sitting on mom's right leg. My youngest brother, Bill, had not been born yet.

As I looked at the photo good memories of the fifties and sixties began to flood my mind. They were good parents and provided a well-disciplined home and life on our small farm. My emotions began to take over and tears welled up in my eyes. So many good times and memories of the years we shared together flashed through my mind.

We lived in the Richland Housing Center until I was about three years old.

My parents worked in the farming community for my mother's father, a peach farmer, and also farmed ten acres of their own peaches. They thinned peaches in the spring, picked peaches in the summer and pruned the trees in the winter. While I was an infant and toddler I stayed in a wooden thirty-five-pound peach lug box during harvest alongside them in the orchard.

When I was about age four we moved to our small farm about one mile east of the Sutter Buttes between Yuba City and Live Oak, California. Most of this farming community was prune and peach orchards. Grain and rice fields were also part of the landscape. My mom quit working in the orchards to care for my brother and me at home. My father continued the orchard work for several more years while also studying agriculture science. He qualified to test and became employed by the Sutter County Agricultural Department where he worked until he retired.

I stayed with my grandfather part of the time during the summer and worked with him on his farm when I was about seven. It was then that he taught me to drive his Ford tractor. I was excited and ecstatic that my grandfather had enough confidence in me to teach me and let me drive his tractor. It was a great experience and opportunity.

Al and I hunted birds with our BB guns and bows and arrows. We played Jack and Bill, which were made up characters. We had our own different make believe ranches. Our vehicles were a red wagon and a red and white tricycle. We had a great amount of fun with these two characters.

We played make believe cowboys and Indians. Each of us had a pair of chaps, a vest, a set of Gene Autry shiny cap guns with holsters and a Roy Rogers lever action plastic cap rifle. We thought we were cool. I have some of these childhood belongings stored away today with other toys I received at Christmas time.

We went fishing in two nearby canals where we caught carp, sunfish and bluegill. The carp were two to five pounds and fun to catch. The sunfish and bluegill were small but tastier. When time allowed we rode our neighbor's horses, Judy and Jolly. How I loved those old horses. When we grew older our parents bought both of us bicycles and we rode with our neighborhood school friends around the surrounding area and in the countryside.

My mom's family lived in this area with her youngest brother living about four miles from our farm. He had a German Shepherd dog named King. Frequently at night King would journey to our farm and wake my brother and I up in the morning by drinking water outside our bedroom window. King was our companion and playmate. He would stay about a week before returning home to my uncle. He continued doing this for several years until he died. This was my first experience with death.

My second death experience was several years later. My first dog was a cute black Cocker Spaniel. She was killed by a car on the street where we lived. After finding her dead on the side of the road, I carried her home, dug a grave, buried her, then made a cross and placed it on her grave along with her collar. Filled with intense grief and a broken heart, I then locked myself in the bathroom and cried until I could cry no more.

Many boys, young and old, and men have been told and believe it is a sign of weakness for them to cry and show their emotions. This is a lie of the enemy, Satan. It is in fact a sign of strength for a man to cry when experiencing grief of any kind. It is actually healthy to cry. It is part of the grieving process and can help us heal. I have known many boys and men who feel crying is a weakness. I have seen that they internalize their grief only to have it negatively affect their health and their relationships with others as it manifests in ways such as anger and bitterness. In the Bible Jesus wept over the death of his friend Lazarus and he wept over Jerusalem.

My youngest brother, Bill, was born in 1956 when I was almost thirteen. When I was about thirteen my family and I went to my grandpa's house to visit. While there I took a pack of my grandpa's cigarettes. After we returned home, my brother Al and I went to a fort we had built in a large grape vine patch. I lit up a cigarette and took a puff, thinking that was cool. We didn't notice our dad and he caught me in the act. He had us come out and took me to grandpa's to return the cigarettes. I returned the cigarettes and said, "I am sorry." When we returned home my dad exercised his parental authority on my behind and I received a serious paddling which heated up the seat of my pants. (I didn't think this was so cool.) This was one of several disciplinary actions I received while living on the farm. I was learning right from wrong.

When I was fourteen the family moved to a house in Sutter, California where my mother became the town's librarian. Life was simple during those years. Living in a small country town we had only a radio so I spent much of my time listening to The Lone Ranger and reading western novels, cowboy books and mysteries. I attribute this time listening to the radio and reading westerns and mysteries to the development of my earnest desire for a cowboy life and law enforcement career. I rode my bicycle around town where I met people and began doing yard work, minor odd jobs and learning my cowboying trade. I always had money in my pocket. I started buying my own clothes, paid for all my activities, purchased my own vehicles and paid all my vehicle expenses.

I began meeting kids in high school, Sutter and the surrounding area. By the time I was sixteen I had many friends. Some of my friends were not walking on the narrow pathway of life. I played sports in high school. If any sports player was caught smoking or drinking alcohol, that person was not allowed to play sports. I had to make decisions about whom I associated with. My parents were strict but loving and helped me choose with whom I would spend my time.

I didn't realize it at the time but I believe in my formative years God's grace also helped direct my behavior. That old expression, "There but for the grace of God go I," has merit. I am thankful for concerned parents and God's grace.

I graduated from Sutter High School in June, 1961. Through the summer I worked in agriculture and cowboy ranch type employment. In the fall of 1961 I worked part time and began classes at Yuba Junior College.

Death Bed Healing

In October, 1961 at age eighteen I experienced flu-like symptoms and couldn't keep any food down. After a week I felt better and like any eighteen-year-old, I went out on the town with my friends. At that time teens and young adults in our area drove "The Cruise" from the Yuba City Bowl to the A&W on Shasta Street and into Marysville. I had a fun weekend and was feeling well. I went back to school at Yuba College on Monday and Tuesday.

Tuesday morning I went home feeling sick to my stomach. My body began to retain water so my mother took me to our family doctor. He told her to take me to the hospital where I was admitted, tests were conducted and it was determined that I had Bright's Disease or Glomerulonephritis, which is a chronic inflammation of the kidneys. It is commonly referred to as Nephritis today. I couldn't keep any medicine or food in my stomach to help me get well. I was beginning to lose consciousness daily. Both of my kidneys stopped functioning. There were no dialysis machines in the Yuba-Sutter area at that time. My prognosis wasn't good. My four doctors told my father I was going to die. There was no hope I would live. I was slipping away and on my way to meet my maker. At the time I was unaware of my condition because my father hadn't told me. I never associated any of my symptoms with death.

In desperation my mother brought in a Methodist pastor from Sutter where I lived and he prayed for me. I vaguely remember him being with me, but I don't recall anything about the prayer. Thanks to God, my kidneys began to function and I started to get better. I regained consciousness, started eating and began feeling better. It was at this point my father told me how critical my condition had been. Two days later I told my doctor I was ready to go home. I wanted to do things and see my friends. He told me to wait a few more days. The doctors were amazed I recovered so quickly. Fourteen days after being admitted, I walked out of the hospital.

With the loss of strength and about twenty pounds, home had a happy ring. Mom's great cooking soon gave me back my strength and my weight, and for the past sixty years I have never had any further kidney problems.

Bright's disease wasn't as treatable in 1961 as it is today. At that time many doctors said death was inevitable. Modern medicine has made huge advancements.

I believe God healed me and raised me from my deathbed. My doctors said death, God said life. Thanks be to God. God is good! I wasn't a Christian at that time but I believed God healed me and saved me from death. I am thankful to the Lord for the extra years He has given me with His many blessings since my near death experience. Praise the Lord!

A Father's Love

I wasn't saved when I was in the hospital with Bright's disease. I do believe my Heavenly Father was watching over me. My earthly father sat by my bedside every day. I always knew he loved my brothers and me. I remember when we were boys he wanted us close. We'd sit on his lap, get hugs and he would read to us.

When I became driving age my dad allowed me to drive the family car around town with my friends. Because I knew he loved me and my mom was concerned about my safety, I was always respectful and let them know when I would be home or coming home late.

As I began thinking about God and salvation I saw a similarity of my earthly father's and God's love. My earthly father sat with me in the hospital because he loved me. My Heavenly Father was looking over me and healed me because He loved me. This realization drew me to a place where I accepted Jesus as my Savior.

God had a plan and purpose for my life. I believe because of the years I have been saved and my years of preparation, God is using me in my current ministry.

We live in a fallen imperfect world and Christians are not exempt from the sorrows of this world. It is God's prerogative to heal or not and deliver us from these tests that come our way. He is gracious, loving, comforting, encouraging and gives us peace. He is a sovereign God. I trust His decisions about my life.

Because of the totality of circumstances in my life, I have grown closer to Him and feel His presence. Praise His Name!

2

BRANDED

Ephesians 1:13b ... *in whom also after that ye believed, ye were sealed with that holy Spirit of promise ... (KJV)*

On occasion while I was growing up I went to church and heard God's word. I had not seriously considered His teachings but after my healing I began to reflect on Him and what He was saying to me. In

1968 while watching Billy Graham on television I gave my life to Jesus (Branded 4 God). I will never forget that day. Thank God for His loving kindness.

Before I was saved I avoided the grace and mercy of God for twenty-six years. I have now served the Lord for over fifty-five years. During this time for approximately twenty-seven years I attended Calvary Temple Assembly of God Church, now Calvary Christian Center and for the past twenty years I have attended Hope Point Nazarene Church. Both churches I have steadily attended are in Yuba City, California.

I have been involved in youth and adult ministry, evangelistic outreach, leadership roles, served fifteen years as an advisory committee leader for a church in Stonyford, California and served several years on the board of directors for the local Salvation Army. Four years I served as a law enforcement chaplain and for the past twenty-two years as a cowboy chaplain. I have conducted cowboy church services at Junior Cowboy Rodeos, High School Rodeos and various other rodeos. For a number of years, I have shared the gospel at other churches, the Twin Cities Rescue Mission, local service organizations and have officiated many funeral services. I have led many home and church bible studies, taught adult Sunday School, led some Wednesday evening services at Calvary Temple and for a number of years have counseled many having personal problems. For several years a good friend and I co-hosted a radio program, "The Christian Cowboy Corral", on a local Christian radio station where we played country gospel songs and shared commentary and personal experiences.

Much of my spiritual training has come from reputable teachers, personal mentors, Bible studies, Berean training through the Assemblies of God, personal study, research from my many commentaries and research books. I have compiled innumerable study notes and prepared many sermons.

I have lived around the Sutter Buttes in Sutter, California and Yuba City, California for my entire life. I grew up in Sutter County; went to Nuestro Grammar School and Sutter High School; graduated from Yuba College with an Associate degree in Administration of Justice; and completed several classes from state colleges. I was employed for about twenty-seven years with the Sutter County Sheriff's Department, working as a deputy sheriff and retiring as a detective sergeant in December, 1999.

It was during the time I was attending Calvary Temple that God did another miracle in my life.

Delivered from Nicotine

In my teenage years I had begun

chewing tobacco. I chewed off and on through those years until it became a habit and I was chewing every day. I began this because I thought it was cool and because of peer pressure from my cowboy friends.

I became a Christian in the latter years of this habit. I was growing in God's grace and knowledge. I began to witness to my friends, my co-workers at the sheriff department and even people I had arrested. God began revealing to me to stop chewing. I struggled with this word from God. I didn't want to stop. I began to realize chewing was harmful to my testimony. I substituted with gum and life savers but they didn't take away my desire. I couldn't stop on my own will power as I was addicted to nicotine. (Wouldn't you think life savers would have delivered me?) I was wrong. I struggled daily for a week. I had such a desire for nicotine.

One Sunday morning I was on my knees in agony. I had decided I wasn't going to church. My wife said something to the effect of, "Come on and go," so I went. I can't remember the content of the sermon but after the sermon was over I went to the altar and dropped to my knees; I began to pray and seek God. All of a sudden the presence of the Lord fell on me. I had a tingling sensation throughout my body and felt the peace and presence of God. I couldn't believe what was happening. I was set free! It felt wonderful. The desire for nicotine was gone and I haven't used any tobacco products since. This happened in 1980, over forty-two years ago.

Now some may say, "Jim, I just had the willpower to quit using tobacco, alcohol or drugs." Be thankful if that was your situation. I wonder where the will power came from. Something to think about. All I know is God blessed you and me.

If anyone reading this has an addiction, seek God, a helpful program or counselor or all three for help. Don't allow a bondage to control your life. God has so much more for you. Take refuge in God.

A Close Call

Working as a deputy, sergeant and detective (During my law enforcement career) I was involved in many types of cases. I investigated many shootings and homicide cases. There were times when armed suspects were at the crime scene, backup had to be called and hopefully would arrive quickly. I prayed for God's grace and protection of all. The cases take many hours to complete and involve suspect interviews, booking of suspects, crime scene investigations, getting the deceased moved to a mortuary and autopsies. Many cases were stressful and I am thankful God was my help and strength.

One incident that occurred during my law enforcement career happened while I was the patrol sergeant on the night shift. A domestic violence call, the most dangerous call for a deputy, came across the radio. Since I and the reserve officer who was riding with me were closest to the location, we responded to the call.

After arriving at the address I parked thirty feet from the driveway then cautiously approached the residence. I had the reserve deputy stay ten feet from the front door to keep watch. We could see the front door was standing open. I approached the front door, knocked and identified myself several times. No one answered. I proceeded in and could see damage to the television and furniture. I cautiously checked the five rooms in the small home. No one was inside so I went outside to look around. Across the street was a row of large trees. I saw a man walk out from behind a tree to the roadside towards me with a machete in his hand. I had my service revolver drawn and told the man several times to drop his machete. He didn't say anything and continued walking towards me. I told him to drop his machete again or I would shoot. He was about ten to twelve feet from me when he stopped, hesitated about a minute then dropped the machete. If he had taken one more step or attempted to raise his machete at me I would have fired my weapon. He was arrested, taken into custody then taken to jail. God has been merciful to me and I thank Him for the many times he protected me.

Accident in the Buttes

I have been riding horses since I was about eleven years old; have worked as a cowboy since I was a teenager and currently still do. I participated in junior rodeo events and team roped for many years. I operated a fifty to eighty cow and steer ranch of my own until 2012. For several ranchers over the last twenty-five years I have managed and cared for five hundred to one thousand head of livestock on six thousand to ten thousand acres each year from November through May in the foothills, the Sutter Buttes and sixteen years on Beale Air Force Base. During the last eight years I have given riding lessons to several girls and coached them for High School Rodeo events.

During my sixty-five years of cowboying, I have had horses fall with me causing many injuries. Both arms, both legs and many ribs have been broken. Both shoulders have been damaged and replaced. I recall several situations when God was watching over me and helped my horse and I get out of mountainous areas to get help. I sometimes question God about some incidents in my life but that is what faith and trust is all about. The Lord has brought me through these accidents with stronger faith. The following is one such accident.

It was a sunny and warm April day. I had gone alone, taking two of my cow dogs with me to check on the cattle in the Sutter Buttes and put out salt for them. I was slowly riding my ATV on a rocky hillside overlooking the cattle in the valley below. I drove my ATV over a large unseen rock with the uphill rear tire. The ATV began to lean towards the downhill side. In an instant I realized the ATV was going to turn over. I decided to jump off so I wouldn't be trapped underneath. My feet landed on the ground but slid out from under me. I landed on an oblong rock about sixteen inches long, twelve inches wide and sticking up about six inches above ground.

My left side and shoulder hit the rock causing intense pain. It felt like I had broken some bones and may have been injured internally. I was in so much pain and could not move. My first thoughts were what do I do now and how am I going to be able to get help. I began to pray and ask the Lord to ease the pain. He granted me that request and also provided His peace. As I began to relax and think clearly I decided to call my wife.

I phoned her and told her what had happened. I asked her to call emergency personnel and the property owner's wife to tell her what happened. Since my wife was unsure as to my location she first called the property owner's wife who then called the rescue personnel. My wife called me back to let me know she had contacted the owner's wife who would call the emergency personnel then she would come to my location. I then called the owner's wife myself and shared the details of my accident and told her my exact location. While waiting for help my two cow dogs stayed with me. They wanted to lick my face and I believe were wondering why I was lying there and not getting up. They lay there with me watching over me. The sun was warm and I was warm and extremely uncomfortable, unable to move lying on the hard ground. I continued praying and talking to the Lord while I waited.

I waited for what seemed like a long time. About thirty minutes later I saw the owner's wife ride her two seater ATV to the base of the hill. She walked up the hill to me. I knew her personally and we visited until some of her family arrived. Rescue personnel then arrived and checked me out. They decided I should be life-flighted to the hospital. While waiting for the helicopter, rescuers put me on a backboard, strapped me to it, put a neck roll on me and took my vitals. That was a painful experience. The helicopter arrived and the medical personnel began their medical review and started an IV with a pain reliever. My pain subsided. They carried me to the helicopter and prepared to load me inside. I teased the medical team and said, "I'm not going to be hanging outside the chopper, am I?" They told me that I would be inside. I also asked how good the pilot was and they explained that he was the best. I trusted their opinion. Just before take-off, I told my dogs to stay and we flew away.

The first rescue team and the flight team were a great group of guys. I knew several of them and they made the ordeal tolerable, jabbing jokes back and forth. The Lord gave me peace and an enjoyable flight.

Prior to me leaving in the helicopter I made arrangements with the owner's wife to take my personal belongings and my dogs for me. Several days later she told me on the phone that my border collies, Tess and Ruby, didn't want to go with her. One of them wanted to lie by my ATV and the other wanted to stay nearby where the helicopter had landed. They were not leaving until the boss returned. She finally was able to persuade them to go with her. They are loyal and faithful working partners. Several of my friends picked up my dogs, ATV, truck and trailer and took them to my home.

I was off work for several weeks. I had five broken ribs and trauma to my rib cage and chest. I now try to be more cautious and observant when riding on a rocky hillside.

Several points I want to make about God's hand in this event....

1. I usually can't make a phone call from the location of my accident because of lack of cell phone reception.

2. I rarely can make phone contact with my wife in the noon hour.

3. Many times, the owner's wife is not home or available to receive phone calls.

4. The Lord relieved my pain and gave me His peace throughout the ordeal.

5. The ATV easily could have rolled on

top of me but it only rolled on its side.

Based on my past experiences it is nearly impossible for all five of these points to happen at the same time. Possibly one of the five, but for all five of them? The Lord had to have a hand in making each of these things happen.

Praise the Lord for His comfort and peace He provided through this ordeal. He is always nearby when I need Him.

Caught off Guard

Most recently in May, 2023 I was in a small corral on the ground loading a cattle truck with seven hundred to eight hundred pound calves when two of them turned back towards me. One of them kicked me in the head causing me to be knocked out for three to four minutes. While I was unconscious one stepped on my chest and the other on my neck and collar bone area. After arriving at the hospital and many tests, the doctors determined there was no brain or internal bleeding. The only injuries I received were many abrasions, a concussion and three broken ribs. I spent three days in the hospital and I am recovering well now at home. The first day in the hospital I had some swelling on my head and a small cut to the left of the left eyebrow where I had been kicked. The cut was glued closed. The second day the swelling on my head was pretty much gone and I had very little bruising on my body. I know God was with me and protected me from sustaining worse or further injuries. Sometimes the choices we make and games we play in life have unforeseen painful consequences causing pain in our lives and others. Thankfully, the prayers of others and the grace of God relieve the pains of life from the games we play and choices we make.

The Lord has helped me through my

life with his grace, comfort and hope. I don't hesitate to cast my cares on Him. I am continually learning to walk in His light. Through the years as a husband, father and grandfather the treasures of wisdom have made an amazing transformation in my life. He guides us through our spiritual journey.

My parents and both of my two brothers who were younger than I have since died. A verse that helps me with them being gone and missing their presence is Psalm 16:11, *You will make known to me the path of life; In Your presence is fullness of joy; In Your right hand there are pleasures forever.* (KJV) This verse is always comforting to me, no matter the circumstances. I believe they are in heaven and one day I will be united with my family and my God.

As Christian believers we face many trials and tests in life. The following chapters have more information and scriptures to help us through some of life's difficult situations. In no way have I tried to answer all questions about man's search and understanding about a Holy God.

3
STORMS OF LIFE

Mark 4:37 *But soon a fierce storm came up. High waves were breaking into the boat, and it began to fill with water. (NLT)*

Storms may happen when Jesus is in our boat and he, most likely, was also wet. He suggested this boat ride!

No one I know wants to go through

any trials and tribulations, it's painful.
Believers may think too many trials in
their life may be because Jesus is not
pleased with them. Not necessarily true,
although it may seem that way. The tests a
believer goes through may be the Holy
Spirit doing spiritual surgery to cut out the
old nature and implant the new nature.

Jesus loves you. The Bible is a spiritual
book. We are spiritual beings. A believer
needs a strong spiritual foundation in their
life.

John 16:33 *"I have told you all this so that
you may have peace in me. Here on earth you will
have many trials and sorrows. But take heart,
because I have overcome the world." (NLT)*

Romans 5:3-5 *We can rejoice, too, when
we run into problems and trials, for we know that
they help us develop endurance. 4 And endurance
develops strength of character, and character
strengthens our confident hope of salvation. 5
And this hope will not lead to disappointment.*

For we know how dearly God loves us, because he has given us the Holy Spirit to fill our hearts with his love. (NLT)

This process helps refine believers and God wouldn't have allowed these tests if there wasn't a purpose. There is also a sequence of how God works in tests. Sometimes, we believers have to be pushed out of our comfort zone to learn. Tests also build character and hope. It is possible some of our tests are designed to work out his plan and purpose for our life. God helps us if we call on Him. Go to God with your concerns. Don't let your heart be troubled. As you successfully pass these tests you will have more faith to pass the next trial in your life. These tests are designed to increase our faith and trust in the Lord.

1 Thessalonians 5:16-18 *Always be joyful. 17 Never stop praying. 18 Be thankful in all circumstances, for this is God's will for you* *who belong to Christ Jesus. (NLT)*

James 1:2-6 *Dear brothers and sisters, when troubles of any kind come your way, consider it an opportunity for great joy. 3 For you know that when your faith is tested, your endurance has a chance to grow. 4 So let it grow, for when your endurance is fully developed, you will be perfect and complete, needing nothing. 5 If you need wisdom, ask our generous God, and he will give it to you. He will not rebuke you for asking. 6 But when you ask him, be sure that your faith is in God alone. Do not waver, for a person with divided loyalty is as unsettled as a wave of the sea that is blown and tossed by the wind. (NLT)*

1 Peter 1:6-7 *So be truly glad. There is a wonderful joy ahead, even though you must endure many trials for a little while. 7 These trials will show that your faith is genuine. It is being tested as fire tests and purifies gold—though your faith is far more precious than mere gold. So when your faith remains strong through many trials, it will* *bring you much praise and glory and honor on the day when Jesus Christ is revealed to the whole world. (NLT)*

Tests and trials come to test our faith. We can endure these trials because of Jesus' help.

John 14:27 *"I am leaving you with a gift— peace of mind and heart. And the peace I give is a gift the world cannot give. So don't be troubled or afraid." (NLT)*

Having peace does not exempt you from trials and conflict, but it will give you a calmness, confidence and sense of courage in God.

1 Corinthians 10:13 *The temptations in your life are no different from what others experience. And God is faithful. He will not allow the temptation to be more than you can stand. When you are tempted, he will show you a way out so that you can endure. (NLT)*

2 Corinthians 1:1-4 *This letter is from Paul, chosen by the will of God to be an apostle of Christ Jesus, and from our brother Timothy.*

I am writing to God's church in Corinth and to all of his holy people throughout Greece. 2 May God our Father and the Lord Jesus Christ give you grace and peace.

God Offers Comfort to All

3 All praise to God, the Father of our Lord Jesus Christ. God is our merciful Father and the source of all comfort. 4 He comforts us in all our troubles so that we can comfort others. When they are troubled, we will be able to give them the same comfort God has given us." (NLT)

Matthew 11:28-29 *Then Jesus said, "Come to me, all of you who are weary and carry heavy burdens, and I will give you rest. 29 Take my yoke upon you. Let me teach you, because I am humble and gentle at heart, and you will find rest for your souls."(NLT)*

In John 10:27, Jesus called his followers sheep. Sheep are not designed to carry a load or a burden. Only donkeys, mules and horses carry loads or work in tandem. Yokes are designed for tandem use on oxen. They are made of wood and fit over the neck of the oxen when cultivating or pulling a wagon. If you are tired and weary carrying your burdens, give them to the Lord.

We need to relax, enjoy God's presence and find rest for our souls. He is always available twenty-four hours a day, seven days a week to help his children.

Romans 8:31b *If God is for us, who can ever be against us? (NLT)*

Romans 15:13 *I pray that God, the source of hope, will fill you completely with joy and peace because you trust in him. Then you will overflow with confident hope through the power of the Holy Spirit. (NLT)*

Most of the time believers would like to live on a mountain top; however to get to the mountain top, we also have to go through the valleys of life. But even mountain tops may appear to be like a rose garden, but be aware of the thorns. Valleys can be life changing, if we choose. That's where the Apostle Paul lived most of his life. Don't allow the valleys to define your life. Keep pressing for the prize, which is Jesus. Paul expressed his perspective on his life adventures in 2 Corinthians 4:8-11.

Everyone is familiar with hurricanes on the east coast. These large storms have in the center what is called the eye of the storm. The eye is about 20-40 miles wide within the middle of the storm. The eye is calm while outside the eye the winds are raging. While you are going through a storm in your life, I suggest you stay in the middle of the storm where it is calm, with the one (I am) who is sovereign over all things.

I think most believers are familiar with the story in Mark 4:35-41, when Jesus suggested that they pass over to the other side of the lake. So they entered the ship and proceeded to the other side. A great wind storm began and waves entered the ship. Jesus was asleep and they awakened him and said they were going to perish. Jesus rebuked the wind and said to the sea, *"Peace, be still."* The wind ceased and it was calm. Why are you so fearful and have no faith? They were afraid and wondered, who is this Man (Jesus) that the sea obeys him?

1. It's interesting that Jesus suggested they enter the ship and go to the other side. Did they think it may not be safe?

2. Sometimes Jesus may wait until the last hour to save His people. (The story of the parting of the Red Sea is a good example of this.)

3. Faith is the answer to fear.

4. Be still in His presence and receive peace.

5. When we pray and call out to Jesus, it is an opportunity for him to respond and answer.

6. Jesus is willing to be in the midst of our storm. Lesson to be learned: no matter the storm, when we get in his presence, there is comfort and peace.

7. If you ride out the storm, you will come out stronger on the other side.

Most vehicles today have a GPS system, their purpose is to give directions and guidance. God's word is our spiritual GPS system. We can draw guidance and strength from His word.

The following scriptures are only a

few that have been helpful to others and to me. I pray they will also be a help to you. Prayerfully study and meditate on them; Look for key words and thoughts of each verse. I believe the Lord will speak to your heart and bless you. Hopefully these scriptures will be a new beginning to encourage you to seek out the treasures of God in your life.

2 Thessalonians 2:16-17 *Now may our Lord Jesus Christ Himself and God our Father, who has loved us and given us eternal comfort and good hope by grace, 17 comfort and strengthen your hearts in every good work and word. (NASB)*

Psalm 1:1-3, 6 *How blessed is the man who does not walk in the counsel of the wicked, Nor stand in the path of sinners, Nor sit in the seat of scoffers! 2 But his delight is in the law of the Lord, And in His law he meditates day and night. 3 He will be like a tree firmly planted by streams of water, Which yields its fruit in its* *season And its leaf does not wither; And in whatever he does, he prospers... 6 For the Lord knows the way of the righteous, But the way of the wicked will perish.*

Psalm 3: 3-5 *But You, O Lord, are a shield about me, My glory, and the One who lifts my head. 4 I was crying to the Lord with my voice, And He answered me from His holy mountain. Selah. 5 I lay down and slept; I awoke, for the Lord sustains me.*

Psalm 16:9-11 *Therefore my heart is glad and my glory rejoices; My flesh also will dwell securely. 10 For You will not abandon my soul to Sheol; Nor will You allow Your Holy One to undergo decay. 11 You will make known to me the path of life; In Your presence is fullness of joy; In Your right hand there are pleasures forever.*

Psalm 18: 2-3 *The Lord is my rock and my fortress and my deliverer, My God, my rock, in whom I take refuge; My shield and the horn of* my salvation, my stronghold. 3 I call upon the Lord, who is worthy to be praised, And I am saved from my enemies.

Psalm 23:4 *Even though I walk through the valley of the shadow of death, I fear no evil, for You are with me; Your rod and Your staff, they comfort me.*

Psalm 27:1 *The LORD is my light and my salvation; Whom shall I fear? The Lord is the defense of my life; Whom shall I dread?*

Psalm 28: 7-8 *The LORD is my strength and my shield; My heart trusts in Him, and I am helped; Therefore my heart exults, And with my song I shall thank Him. 8 The LORD is their strength, And He is a saving defense to His anointed.*

Psalm 32:8 *I will instruct you and teach you in the way which you should go; I will counsel you with My eye upon you.*

Psalm 34:1-4 *I will bless the LORD at all times; His praise shall continually be in my mouth. 2 My soul will make its boast in the LORD; The humble will hear it and rejoice. 3 O magnify the LORD with me, And let us exalt His name together. 4 I sought the LORD, and He answered me, And delivered me from all my fears.*

Psalm 34:13-17 *Keep your tongue from evil And your lips from speaking deceit. 14 Depart from evil and do good; Seek peace and pursue it. 15 The eyes of the LORD are toward the righteous And His ears are open to their cry. 16 The face of the LORD is against evildoers, To cut off the memory of them from the earth. 17 The righteous cry, and the LORD hears And delivers them out of all their troubles.*

Psalm 37:3-9 *Trust in the LORD and do good; Dwell in the land and cultivate faithfulness. 4 Delight yourself in the LORD; And He will give you the desires of your heart. 5 Commit your way to the LORD, Trust also in Him, and He* will do it. 6 *He will bring forth your righteousness as the light And your judgment as the noonday. 7 Rest in the LORD and wait patiently for Him; Do not fret because of him who prospers in his way, Because of the man who carries out wicked schemes. 8 Cease from anger and forsake wrath; Do not fret; it leads only to evildoing. 9 For evildoers will be cut off, But those who wait for the LORD, they will inherit the land.*

Psalm 37:23-26 *The steps of a man are established by the LORD, And He delights in his way. 24 When he falls, he will not be hurled headlong, Because the LORD is the One who holds his hand. 25 I have been young and now I am old, Yet I have not seen the righteous forsaken Or his descendants begging bread. 26 All day long he is gracious and lends, And his descendants are a blessing.*

Psalm 40:1-4 *I waited patiently for the LORD; And He inclined to me and heard my cry. 2 He brought me up out of the pit of destruction, out of the miry clay, And He set my* *feet upon a rock making my footsteps firm. 3 He put a new song in my mouth, a song of praise to our God; Many will see and fear And will trust in the LORD. 4 How blessed is the man who has made the LORD his trust, And has not turned to the proud, nor to those who lapse into falsehood.*

Psalm 42:5 *Why are you in despair, O my soul? And why have you become disturbed within me? Hope in God,or I shall again praise Him For the help of His presence.*

Psalm 51:1-4 *Be gracious to me, O God, according to Your lovingkindness; According to the greatness of Your compassion blot out my transgressions. 2 Wash me thoroughly from my iniquity And cleanse me from my sin. 3 For I know my transgressions, And my sin is ever before me. 4 Against You, You only, I have sinned And done what is evil in Your sight, So that You are justified when You speak And blameless when You judge.*

Psalm 62:5-8 *My soul, wait in silence for God only, For my hope is from Him. 6 He only is my rock and my salvation, My stronghold; I shall not be shaken. 7 On God my salvation and my glory rest; The rock of my strength, my refuge is in God. 8 Trust in Him at all times, O people; Pour out your heart before Him; God is a refuge for us. Selah*

Psalm 63:1-3 *O God, You are my God; I shall seek You earnestly; My soul thirsts for You, my flesh yearns for You, In a dry and weary land where there is no water. 2 Thus I have seen You in the sanctuary, To see Your power and Your glory. 3 Because Your lovingkindness is better than life, My lips will praise You.*

Psalm 84:11 *For the LORD God is a sun and shield; The Lord gives grace and glory; No good thing does He withhold from those who walk uprightly.*

Psalm 91:14-16 *"Because he has loved Me, therefore I will deliver him; I will set him* *securely on high, because he has known My name. 15 "He will call upon Me, and I will answer him; I will be with him in trouble; I will rescue him and honor him. 16 "With a long life I will satisfy him And let him see My salvation."*

Psalm 103:1-5 *Bless the LORD, O my soul, And all that is within me, bless His holy name. 2 Bless the LORD, O my soul, And forget none of His benefits; 3 Who pardons all your iniquities, Who heals all your diseases; 4 Who redeems your life from the pit, Who crowns you with lovingkindness and compassion; 5 Who satisfies your years with good things, So that your youth is renewed like the eagle.*

Psalm 118: 5-8 *From my distress I called upon the LORD; The LORD answered me and set me in a large place. 6 The LORD is for me; I will not fear; What can man do to me? 7 The LORD is for me among those who help me; Therefore I will look with satisfaction on those who hate me. 8 It is better to take refuge in the LORD Than to trust in man.*

Psalm 118:14 *The LORD is my strength and song, And He has become my salvation.*

Psalm 119: 67-68 *Before I was afflicted I went astray, But now I keep Your word. 68 You are good and do good; Teach me Your statutes.*

Psalm 119:105 *Your word is a lamp to my feet And a light to my path.*

Psalm 139: 14-18 *I will give thanks to You, for I am fearfully and wonderfully made; Wonderful are Your works, And my soul knows it very well. 15 My frame was not hidden from You, When I was made in secret, And skillfully wrought in the depths of the earth; 16 Your eyes have seen my unformed substance; And in Your book were all written The days that were ordained for me, When as yet there was not one of them. 17 How precious also are Your thoughts to me, O God! How vast is the sum of them! 18 If I should count them, they would outnumber the sand. When I awake, I am still with You.*

Psalm 139: 23-24 *Search me, O God, and know my heart; Try me and know my anxious thoughts; 24 And see if there be any hurtful way in me, And lead me in the everlasting way.*

Psalm 147: 1-3 *Praise the LORD! For it is good to sing praises to our God; For it is pleasant and praise is becoming. 2 The LORD builds up Jerusalem; He gathers the outcasts of Israel. 3 He heals the brokenhearted And binds up their wounds.*

Psalm 150:1-2 *Praise the LORD! Praise God in His sanctuary; Praise Him in His mighty expanse. 2 Praise Him for His mighty deeds; Praise Him according to His excellent greatness.*

Proverbs 3:5-8 *Trust in the LORD with all your heart And do not lean on your own understanding. 6 In all your ways acknowledge Him, And He will make your paths straight. 7*

Do not be wise in your own eyes; Fear the LORD and turn away from evil. 8 It will be healing to your body And refreshment to your bones.

Proverbs 3:11-13 *My son, do not reject the discipline of the LORD Or loathe His reproof, 12 For whom the LORD loves He reproves, Even as a father corrects the son in whom he delights. 13 How blessed is the man who finds wisdom And the man who gains understanding.*

Proverbs 4:20-23 *My son, give attention to my words; Incline your ear to my sayings. 21 Do not let them depart from your sight; Keep them in the midst of your heart. 22 For they are life to those who find them And health to all their body. 23 Watch over your heart with all diligence, For from it flow the springs of life.*

Proverbs 23:12 *Apply your heart to discipline And your ears to words of knowledge.*

Isaiah 41:10 *Do not fear, for I am with you; Do not anxiously look about you, for I am your God. I will strengthen you, surely I will help you, Surely I will uphold you with My righteous right hand.*

Isaiah 41:13 *For I am the Lord your God, who upholds your right hand, Who says to you, "Do not fear, I will help you."*

1 Peter 5:6-11 *Therefore humble yourselves under the mighty hand of God, that He may exalt you at the proper time, 7 casting all your anxiety on Him, because He cares for you. 8 Be of sober spirit, be on the alert. Your adversary, the devil, prowls around like a roaring lion, seeking someone to devour. 9 But resist him, firm in your faith, knowing that the same experiences of suffering are being accomplished by your brethren who are in the world. 10 After you have suffered for a little while, the God of all grace, who called you to His eternal glory in Christ, will Himself perfect, confirm, strengthen and establish you. 11 To Him be dominion forever and ever.*

Amen.

Notice the word does not say the devil is a lion, but like a lion. His actions are similar to a lion seeking for prey to devour. If you believe Satan is tempting you, stand firm in your faith. God will strengthen you.

Have you ever had any of these thoughts while you or others are in a storm? Why is there no immediate help from God? When I pray for someone sick, why are they not healed? Prayers for finances, feelings of despair, loneliness, longsuffering and anxiousness seem to go unanswered. I do not have peace or hope. Others appear to be doing well, but not me. It is like God is not listening to my prayers. When I do pray, I feel like I am knocking on the door of Heaven and no one is home. Am I on a heavenly waiting list and it is not my turn?

I believe all of us may have felt this way at some time in our lives. Many in

Bible history have been in situations where they probably had such thoughts: Joseph who for years went through many tests before he was exalted to the second highest position in Egypt; Sarah who was past the age to have children when God promised her a son waited years for her promised son, Isaac, to be born; Moses was a shepherd for forty years before God called him to deliver His people out of Egypt.

In Hebrews chapter 11 is a list of those who were faithful. In verses 36-40 many of the faithful experienced scourging, imprisonment, were stoned, were put to death, lived in caves, not receiving the promise before dying. These saints still kept the faith even though they suffered immensely. They were looking for a heavenly city and a better country. God was pleased with them and they finally received their reward.

I don't know the plans and purposes of God for each of His saints. But, I do know and believe that whatever His plan is, we should keep the faith, trust and have hope. Our hope will ultimately be rewarded when we pass from this life to that heavenly country.

The following scripture may describe how you feel:

Psalm 44:23-26 *Arouse Yourself, why do You sleep, O Lord? Awake, do not reject us forever. 24 Why do You hide Your face And forget our affliction and our oppression? 25 For our soul has sunk down into the dust; Our body cleaves to the earth. 26 Rise up, be our help, And redeem us for the sake of Your lovingkindness.*

However, don't grow weary of doing good. One day you will be rewarded for your faith in God.

Ephesians 3:16-17 *"… hat He would grant you, according to the riches of His glory, to be strengthened with power through His Spirit in the inner man, 17 so that Christ may dwell in* *your hearts through faith; and that you, being rooted and grounded in love …*

Remember He chose you before the foundation of the world. He has promised you eternal life. God has filled you with His presence and you are His earthly home. (1 Corinthians 3:16) Don't lose hope. One day you will be living in a new heaven and earth with Him; No more pain, sorrow and tears.

If you are searching for help, answers, encouragement and hope from the Lord, seek Him diligently and pray. In His timing He will give you strength, comfort and peace from His word. May His mercy and grace be sufficient for all your needs. You are unique, special and the apple of His eye. So, step out of the valley of shadows and into His marvelous light and smile… Jesus loves you.

4

SALVATION

John 3:15 ... *so that whoever believes will in Him have eternal life.*

I am opening this chapter with a quote from Donald Grey Barnhouse's book "Revelation God's Last Word", published by Zondervan in 1972, page 97. "The stary host of heaven never cease to proclaim God's majesty and glory. By day the sun by night the moon and the stars speak of Him. And as the heavens declare the glory of God, so the angelic hosts "rest not day nor night." Men have turned away from God and have followed one of the cherubim into rebellion. The earth bears the mark of the curse upon sin. Yet God will be worshiped and his creation, animate and inanimate, will continue to praise Him."

2 Corinthians 9:15 *Thanks be to God for His indescribable gift!*

2 Corinthians 5:21 *He made Him who knew no sin to be sin on our behalf, so that we might become the righteousness of God in Him.*

The theme of the bible is a heavenly message to the world - looking forward to Jesus and the cross. Salvation is available to all who call on His name. Man needed a savior because of our sin nature.

Because of the fall in Genesis 3 all have been born under the kingdom of darkness which is ruled by Satan. The kingdom of light is ruled by Jesus who is the light of the world. Jesus has brought us out of darkness into His light because of his death on the cross. The cross changed the world's darkness to light.

Colossians 1:12-14 … *giving thanks to the Father, who has qualified us to share in the inheritance of the saints in Light.13 For He rescued us from the domain of darkness, and transferred us to the kingdom of His beloved Son, 14 in whom we have redemption, the forgiveness of sins.*

So when we are born into this world (natural birth) we are born into spiritual darkness. When we are born of the spirit or born from above we are born into the spiritual light. We have been set free from the power of sin and death.

Hebrews 2:14-15 *Therefore, since the children share in flesh and blood, He Himself* *likewise also partook of the same, that through death He might render powerless him who had the power of death, that is, the devil, 15 and might free those who through fear of death were subject to slavery all their lives.*

2 Timothy 1:9-10 *... who has saved us and called us with a holy calling, not according to our works, but according to His own purpose and grace which was granted us in Christ Jesus from all eternity, 10 but now has been revealed by the appearing of our Savior Christ Jesus, who abolished death and brought life and immortality to light through the gospel ...*

Jesus and the cross brought hope of eternal life to mankind. All your sins have been paid for. He is the anchor of our soul. Solid, sure and true. The power of death doesn't have a hold on us anymore once we allow Him into our lives. Faith has given us access to the righteousness of God, but Satan wants to steal you away from His righteousness.

John 10:10 *"The thief comes only to steal and kill and destroy; I came that they may have life, and have it abundantly."*

John 1:4 *In Him was life, and the life was the light of men.*

A word about abundant life. Satan is always trying to deceive one not to believe in God's word. Jesus is encouraging us to believe. The abundant life demands us to continue to believe God's word during our Christian life. Obedience is the key to abundant life.

Many times we read or hear the word and choose not to obey. The result is not reaping the abundant life. Satan is a liar, crook and murderer.

John 8:44 *"You are of your father the devil, and you want to do the desires of your father. He was a murderer from the beginning, and does not stand in the truth because there is no* *truth in him. Whenever he speaks a lie, he speaks from his own nature, for he is a liar and the father of lies."*

We have been created by God with free will giving us a choice to obediently follow Him and spiritually receive the fullness of His word.

1 Peter 1:19-21 ... *but with precious blood, as of a lamb unblemished and spotless, the blood of Christ. 20 For He was foreknown before the foundation of the world, but has appeared in these last times for the sake of you 21 who through Him are believers in God, who raised Him from the dead and gave Him glory, so that your faith and hope are in God.*

So now we are children of light, born again, spirit filled and heaven bound.

Jesus was born into an unrepentant world. He went to the cross to show his love and the Father's love for mankind. Man needed a savior and Jesus was that man. When He was on the cross we were on His mind. AMEN.

The following scriptures will introduce you to God's plan of salvation.

Romans 3:23 ... *for all have sinned and fall short of the glory of God* ...

Your only hope of being freed from sin is faith in Jesus.

Romans 6:23 *For the wages of sin is death, but the free gift of God is eternal life in Christ Jesus our Lord.*

If we live in unbelief, we are still living in the kingdom of darkness. If we reject Jesus, we are refusing his salvation. No matter how good you are, you are spiritually dead and you have no hope of eternal life without Christ. Hell will be where you will spend your afterlife. It is the absence of God. My prayer for you is you will reconsider your decision.

Ephesians 2:1 *And you were dead in your trespasses and sins …*

John 3:5-6 *Jesus answered, "Truly, truly, I say to you, unless one is born of water and the Spirit he cannot enter into the kingdom of God. 6 That which is born of the flesh is flesh, and that which is born of the Spirit is spirit."*

John 3:16-21 *"For God so loved the world, that He gave His only begotten Son, that whoever believes in Him shall not perish, but have eternal life. 17 For God did not send the Son into the world to judge the world, but that the world might be saved through Him. 18 He who believes in Him is not judged; he who does not believe has been judged already, because he has not believed in the name of the only begotten Son of God. 19 This is the judgment, that the Light has come into the world, and men loved the darkness rather than the Light, for their deeds were evil. 20 For everyone who does evil hates the Light, and does not come to the Light for fear that his deeds will* *be exposed. 21 But he who practices the truth comes to the Light, so that his deeds may be manifested as having been wrought in God.'"*

Several points about His death:

1. It demonstrates the seriousness of sin and God's immeasurable love.

2. Jesus was raised from the dead. He demonstrated to doubting Thomas by showing him His nail scarred hands and feet and told him to put his hand in His side.

3. Jesus told His listeners He would be raised from the dead.

4. After His resurrection He was seen by over 500 people at one time during the 40 days He was still on earth and before His ascension.

5. Salvation is available to whoever will

believe. If one doesn't believe, they will perish. We only have two choices - believe or perish.

6. Jesus doesn't judge or condemn. A person condemns themselves because they prefer darkness to light.

Romans 10:9 … *that if you confess with your mouth Jesus as Lord, and believe in your heart that God raised Him from the dead, you will be saved.*

Acts 3:19 *Therefore repent and return, so that your sins may be wiped away, in order that times of refreshing may come from the presence of the Lord …*

Repentance brings times of refreshing from the presence of the Lord. Confession is good for the soul.

All of us will be judged on our works. Christians won't be judged on our bad works but on our good works. Non believers will be judged on their works because they have rejected Jesus. Don't miss out on salvation, believe and be rewarded.

1 John 5:11-13 *And the testimony is this, that God has given us eternal life, and this life is in His Son. 12 He who has the Son has the life; he who does not have the Son of God does not have the life. 13 These things I have written to you who believe in the name of the Son of God, so that you may know that you have eternal life.*

Hebrews 12:2 *"Fixing our eyes on Jesus, the author and perfecter of faith, who for the joy set before Him endured the cross, despising the shame, and has sat down at the right hand of the throne of God."*

Titus 3:5 *… he saved us, not on the basis of deeds which we have done in righteousness, but according to His mercy, by the washing of regeneration and renewing by the Holy Spirit …*

Jesus didn't die on the cross because we are such good people but because we are sinners. You and I are the reason Jesus went to the cross.

Do you comprehend how long you were in God's thoughts before He died for you? Ephesians 1:4 states "before the foundation of the world".

Ephesians 5:8 ... *for you were formerly darkness, but now you are Light in the Lord; walk as children of light* ...

Colossians 2:13-14 *When you were dead in your transgressions and the uncircumcision of your flesh, He made you alive together with Him, having forgiven us all our transgressions, 14 having canceled out the certificate of debt consisting of decrees against us, which was hostile to us; and He has taken it out of the way, having nailed it to the cross.*

Ephesians 1:3-4 *Blessed be the God and Father of our Lord Jesus Christ, who has blessed* us with every spiritual blessing in the heavenly places in Christ, 4 just as He chose us in Him before the foundation of the world, that we would be holy and blameless before Him.

1 Peter 2:9 *But you are A CHOSEN RACE, A ROYAL PRIESTHOOD, A HOLY NATION, A PEOPLE FOR God's OWN POSSESSION, so that you may proclaim the excellencies of Him who has called you out of darkness into His marvelous light;*

Peter states a believer is a "chosen race." You are special because of His love and He has chosen you to receive His precious endowment of love free of charge. When your old nature is dying you are allowing God to be fruitful in your life. It is called the surrendered life.

God's gift of salvation is a free gift. When one believes, God removes sin from us and gives the goodness of God to us. This allows a believer to stand before God just as if one never sinned.

Believers are now part of a royal priesthood. I can't wait until I am welcomed home at the foot of His throne.

Note: A Christian's heart demonstrates the love of God. The heart is a part of our inner being. Proverbs 4:23 states that out of our heart "flow the springs of life." Our heart should reflect God's love and goodness. However, there are times we may stumble and say or do something that is ungodly. When that happens we need to confess our sin to God and ask him to cleanse our heart and soul.

1 John 1:9 *If we confess our sins, He is faithful and righteous to forgive us our sins and to cleanse us from all unrighteousness.*

Romans 10:13 *For "WHOEVER WILL CALL ON THE NAME OF THE LORD WILL BE SAVED."*

Notice that anyone who calls on His name shall be saved. God is inclusive of all men with his salvation. Call on the name of the Lord, give up your selfish ways and lay up treasures in heaven.

Hebrews 13:20-21 *Now the God of peace, who brought up from the dead the great Shepherd of the sheep through the blood of the eternal covenant, even Jesus our Lord, 21 equip you in every good thing to do His will, working in us that which is pleasing in His sight, through Jesus Christ, to whom be the glory forever and ever. Amen.*

I believe the gospel of salvation is one of the themes in the Bible. Jesus and the Father loved us because we are his creation and we needed a redeemer. The cross was a painful way to die. It caused pain for Jesus and the Father. I believe it was love that kept Jesus on the cross and not the nails.

Romans 5:8 *But God demonstrates His own love toward us, in that while we were yet sinners, Christ died for us.*

Picture in your mind the rugged cross at Calvary. Jesus was hung on that cross. Jesus was God incarnate, God in the flesh. He was spat on, his body was beaten, bruised and bloody from His head to His feet. A crown of thorns was put on His head by the soldiers. A spear was thrust in His side to insure He was dead. Blood and water came out. Jesus was dead.

The blood He shed was to cover the sin of mankind. This act was the final sacrifice for sin. The scripture states in Revelation 13:8, Jesus was *the Lamb slain from the foundation of the world.* (KJV) This is an amazing scripture, that in the foreknowledge and predetermined plan of the Father He had this plan for the redemption of man's sin. It took the perfect person (the clean) to redeem the unperfect (the unclean) to save us. He offers salvation and eternal life to whoever will call on His name and accept Him by faith. Praise God!

A word about truth: Pilate, the man who turned Jesus over to be crucified turned to Jesus and asked, "What is truth?" Jesus said, "I have come to the world to testify to the truth." (NASB)

Here is a simple definition drawn from what the Bible teaches: Truth is that which is consistent with the mind, will, character, glory and being of God. Truth is the self-expression of God. Therefore, God is the author, source, determiner, governor, arbiter, ultimate standard and final judge of all truth. The Old Testament refers to the Almighty as the God of Truth.

Deuteronomy 32:4 *"The Rock! His work is perfect, For all His ways are just; God of faithfulness and without injustice, Righteous and upright is He."*

Jesus said the written word of God is truth.

John 14:6 *Jesus said to him, "I am the way, and the truth, and the life; no one comes to the Father but through Me."*

He is the way because He is truth and life.

John 14:10 *"Do you not believe that I am in the Father, and the Father is in Me? The words that I say to you I do not speak on My own initiative, but the Father abiding in Me does His works."*

Jesus is carrying out the work of the Father. There are many more scriptures that declare truth. If He created all things, is supreme over all things and holds all creation together should one not trust Him for the truth of salvation?

Colossians 1:15-17 *He is the image of*

the invisible God, the firstborn of all creation. 16 For by Him all things were created, both in the heavens and on earth, visible and invisible, whether thrones or dominions or rulers or authorities—all things have been created through Him and for Him. 17 He is before all things, and in Him all things hold together.

Need I say anything more. Jesus was born into a lost disgruntled world of turmoil with lonely, depressed, anxious, unsatisfied sinful people when things seemed hopeless. When He was raised from the dead He provided a new way to live full of mercy, grace, love, peace, forgiveness and hope.

Gilbert. K. Chesterton, Catholic theologian, philosopher and writer, states, "To love means loving the unlovable. To forgive means pardoning the unpardonable. Faith means believing the unbelievable. Hope means hoping when everything seems hopeless."

Revelation 3:20-21 *"Behold, I stand at the door and knock; if anyone hears My voice and opens the door, I will come in to him and will dine with him, and he with Me. 21 He who overcomes, I will grant to him to sit down with Me on My throne, as I also overcame and sat down with My Father on His throne."*

We read that Jesus is knocking at the door but we have to open the door. Jesus will not kick open the door, we have to open it. It is our duty to allow Jesus in our life. Don't miss the opportunity of a lifetime of blessings.

Before I provide a prayer of salvation I want to say a few words about heaven. Heaven is a place of beauty beyond comprehension. It is beyond description and amazing. No more death, pain, suffering, sorrow, tears and the trials we face here on earth. A place of peace, joy, happiness and enjoying the presence and glory of the Father, Son and Holy Spirit.

Those who enter will be excited they chose Jesus. Believers will enjoy the fullness of God, the mansion that's being prepared for us and an evening stroll with Jesus on the streets of gold. There won't be any charge for electricity, power or food. Jesus, the light of the world, is the light. There is a river which flows from God's throne and the tree of life are for food and healing. If you like adventures, heaven is one place you don't want to miss. It will be beyond your imagination.

If you are not a believer or want to rededicate your life to Jesus, the following sincere prayer will secure a place in the Lamb's (Jesus) book of life. The angels will rejoice in heaven when you trust Jesus for salvation.

Salvation Prayer

Lord Jesus, I turn from my sins and believe you died for my sins. I believe in my heart that God raised you from the dead and if I call on your name I will be saved. I ask for forgiveness and receive you into my life and heart as my Lord and Savior. Amen.

If you sincerely prayed the above prayer and believe, you are saved. The stage is now set for a new exciting life.

Isaiah 43:25 *"I, even I, am the one who wipes out your transgressions for My own sake, And I will not remember your sins."*

However, it doesn't make any difference today where you were born, your ethnic background or nationality. It is whether you believe in Jesus.

I believe this is plenty of evidence that demonstrates God and His word are true. It is a fresh look at a new life. So open your heart to God. Thanks be to the Father, Son and Holy Spirit for their mercy, grace, love and truth.

The thought in your mind should now raise this question. Do I accept His offer of new life or reject His offer of love?

Jesus did His part on the cross so we should live for Him by grace and truth. After all, relationships are built on love. So salvation is a heart to heart love affair with God. Eternal life is now available for all who believe. I can't believe He saved me, a man made of dirt, from sin. I am so thankful for salvation. He paid my entry fee into Heaven. It is free! I have citizenship in heaven.

5

FAITH IN ACTION

1 Samuel 17:29-37 *And David said, What have I now done?* <u>*Is there not a cause?*</u> *30 And he turned from him toward another, and spake after the same manner: and the people answered him again after the former manner.*

31 And when the words were heard which David spake, they rehearsed them before Saul: and he sent for him. 32 And

David said to Saul, Let no man's heart fail because of him; thy servant will go and fight with this Philistine. 33 And Saul said to David, Thou art not able to go against this Philistine to fight with him: for thou art but a youth, and he a man of war from his youth. 34 And David said unto Saul, Thy servant kept his father's sheep, and there came a lion, and a bear, and took a lamb out of the flock: 35 and I went out after him, and smote him, and delivered it out of his mouth: and when he arose against me, I caught him by his beard, and smote him, and slew him. 36 Thy servant slew both the lion and the bear: and this uncircumcised Philistine shall be as one of them, seeing he hath defied the armies of the living God. 37 David said moreover, The LORD that delivered me out of the paw of the lion, and out of the paw of the bear, he will deliver me out of the hand of this Philistine. And Saul said unto David, Go, and the LORD be with thee. (KJV)

As we read in 1 Samuel 17 we find the Philistine army in a battle with Israel. The enemy, Goliath, has God's people held hostage and in a state of fear keeping them from being the people God called them to be.

Deuteronomy 31:6 *"Be strong and courageous, do not be afraid or tremble at them, for the Lord your God is the one who goes with you. He will not fail you or forsake you."*

No one has the courage to step up to the task of killing the giant. However a young lad named David arrived on the scene with some goodies for his brothers. After being briefed about Goliath he had a conversation with King Saul. David was determined he could take out Goliath. David said to Saul he had confidence he could kill the giant. So David took his weapon of choice, a slingshot and five smooth stones. David and Goliath had a challenging conversation. Ultimately they faced off and David killed Goliath with his sling demonstrating to the enemy that the battle was the Lord's. The enemy was overcome and fled. When the Lord has prepared one for a spiritual battle we can be victorious and overcomers.

Romans 15:4 *For whatever was written in earlier times was written for our instruction, so that through perseverance and the encouragement of the Scriptures we might have hope.*

The next verses admonish us to avoid some of the mistakes Israel made.

1 Corinthians 10:11-13 *Now these things happened to them as an example, and they were written for our instruction, upon whom the ends of the ages have come. 12 Therefore let him who thinks he stands take heed that he does not fall. 13 No temptation has overtaken you but such as is common to man; and God is faithful, who will not allow you to be tempted beyond what you are* able, but with the temptation will provide the way of escape also, so that you will be able to endure it.

Life in the wilderness of old is typical of the Christian life. Believers are always being tested by faith. All the obedient Old Testament believers lived by faith. Abraham trusted and believed God.

Romans 4:3 *For what does the Scripture say? "Abraham believed God, and it was credited to him as righteousness."*

Deuteronomy 8:2-3 *"You shall remember all the way which the Lord your God has led you in the wilderness these forty years, that He might humble you, testing you, to know what was in your heart, whether you would keep His commandments or not. 3 He humbled you and let you be hungry, and fed you with manna which you did not know, nor did your fathers know, that He might make you understand that man does not live by bread alone, but man lives by everything* *that proceeds out of the mouth of the Lord."*

I believe these verses and others teach we will be tested but we should trust Jesus and walk in faith. Obedience and faith bring forth spiritual blessings and protection.

In Matthew 14:22-31 Jesus told his disciples to get in a ship and go to the other side and the wind became furious.

Matthew 14:22-31 *Immediately He made the disciples get into the boat and go ahead of Him to the other side, while He sent the crowds away. 23 After He had sent the crowds away, He went up on the mountain by Himself to pray; and when it was evening, He was there alone. 24 But the boat was already a long distance from the land, battered by the waves; for the wind was contrary. 25 And in the fourth watch of the night He came to them, walking on the sea. 26 When the disciples saw Him walking on the sea, they were terrified, and said, "It is a ghost!" And*

*they cried out in fear. 27 But immediately Jesus
spoke to them, saying, "Take courage, it is I; do
not be afraid."*

*28 Peter said to Him, "Lord, if it is You,
command me to come to You on the water." 29
And He said, "Come!" And Peter got out of the
boat, and walked on the water and came toward
Jesus. 30 But seeing the wind, he became
frightened, and beginning to sink, he cried out,
"Lord, save me!" 31 Immediately Jesus stretched
out His hand and took hold of him, and said to
him, "You of little faith, why did you doubt?"*

Notice Jesus told the disciples to get
in the boat and go to the other side. So
away they go and the boat is tossing and
turning and they are scared. Jesus comes
walking on the water and says be of good
cheer. "It is I." Be not afraid. Before this
time no one had walked on water. Peter
made a bold request. Can I come and
Jesus said, "Come". Peter began his walk
and got his eyes off Jesus and Jesus had to
rescue him. Moral of the story - if we

know Jesus is near, we need not be afraid. Keep your eyes on Jesus. Jesus doesn't panic in storms of life. Also when you get a word or verse from God as Peter did when going through a test don't lose your focus and use your wisdom to resolve your problem.

Believers must stand for truth and values against our enemy. We should also stand for our faith and be bold. He is our deliverer.

Acts 4:11-12 *"He is the stone which was rejected by you, the builders, but which became the chief corner stone. 12 And there is salvation in no one else; for there is no other name under heaven that has been given among men by which we must be saved."*

Is there still a cause as in David's day? Yes. As mentioned earlier in this book, the Christian life is not a rose garden. Thorns are alive and well. The seas of life can be scary. The mountains are high and the valleys are low. Sometimes the valley can be so low it seems as though we may be drowning.

This wilderness life is something we all experience. It is not a fun place to be but it is a place of testing and development of our spiritual life. It is easy to give up and not trust God. But He is working on our inner man and doing something new in your life. Remember He directs our path step by step, so stay on the path. He is going before us so trust and follow. No matter whether it is spiritual, emotional, an illness, great doubt or we have caused the problem, we must wait and trust the Lord. He will provide and answer. Allow the process to come to completion and increase your faith and hope. Yes there shall be mountains to be moved but have faith. Jesus said if you have faith as a mustard seed you can say to the mountain, be removed. These mountains are not literal but spiritual. By faith God can do all things.

1 Peter 1:6-7 *In this you greatly rejoice, even though now for a little while, if necessary, you have been distressed by various trials, 7 so that the proof of your faith, being more precious than gold which is perishable, even though tested by fire, may be found to result in praise and glory and honor at the revelation of Jesus Christ.*

We can't control the circumstances we are given in life. All we can do is decide whether we will let them control us. When we experience these trials we need to be joyful. God has a plan and purpose to strengthen our lives. Don't let Jesus walk by you when you have a need. Be like the woman that had an issue of blood. Reach out, touch him and receive a blessing. (Matthew 9:20-22) So live in His presence and don't grow weary of doing good.

Ecclesiastes 3:1 *There is an appointed time for everything. And there is a time for every event under heaven:*

Nahum 1:7 *The Lord is good, A stronghold in the day of trouble, And He knows those who take refuge in Him.*

Psalm 55:22 *Cast your burden upon the Lord and He will sustain you; He will never allow the righteous to be shaken.*

When we go through trials we are being strengthened.

Not everyone can be a Jesse who provided food and support for his sons nor a David as an instrument prepared by God to take out Goliath. Don't look upon yourself as one NOT capable if God has called you. I have found God has usually prepared me to face unforeseen trials most of the time or given me a good word. There are many needs within the body of Christ where help is needed.

In Romans Paul wrote about gifts of service to be used by believers in the church.

Romans 12:4-13 *For just as we have many members in one body and all the members do not have the same function, 5 so we, who are many, are one body in Christ, and individually members one of another. 6 Since we have gifts that differ according to the grace given to us, each of us is to exercise them accordingly: if prophecy, according to the proportion of his faith; 7 if service, in his serving; or he who teaches, in his teaching; 8 or he who exhorts, in his exhortation; he who gives, with liberality; he who leads, with diligence; he who shows mercy, with cheerfulness.*

9 Let love be without hypocrisy. Abhor what is evil; cling to what is good. 10 Be devoted to one another in brotherly love; give preference to one another in honor; 11 not lagging behind in diligence, fervent in spirit, serving the Lord; 12 rejoicing in hope, persevering in tribulation, devoted to prayer, 13 contributing to the needs of the saints, practicing hospitality.

It is important these gifts are used for the church to function as God would like;

all of the congregation has to be involved.

1 Corinthians 12 also defines many spiritual gifts to be used correctly when a congregation meets. Paul lists many members of the body parts that are useful in service to the Lord. In verse 20 Paul states, "there are many members, but one body." Paul writes there should "be no division in the body" but that we should care for one another. He also states that the weaker members are necessary. Weaker members are susceptible to injury, are feeble, not as strong or have internal medical problems. God will use anyone who is willing.

James 1:27 *Pure and undefiled religion in the sight of our God and Father is this: to visit orphans and widows in their distress, and to keep oneself unstained by the world.*

1 Timothy 5:1-3 *Do not sharply rebuke an older man, but rather appeal to him as a father, to the younger men as brothers, 2 the older* women as mothers, and the younger women as sisters, in all purity. 3 Honor widows who are widows indeed.

A widow must be above reproach. Families are also responsible for their family members who are needy.

Matthew 25:34-40 *"Then the King will say to those on His right, 'Come, you who are blessed of My Father, inherit the kingdom prepared for you from the foundation of the world. 35 For I was hungry, and you gave Me something to eat; I was thirsty, and you gave Me something to drink; I was a stranger, and you invited Me in; 36 naked, and you clothed Me; I was sick, and you visited Me; I was in prison, and you came to Me.' 37 Then the righteous will answer Him, 'Lord, when did we see You hungry, and feed You, or thirsty, and give You something to drink? 38 And when did we see You a stranger, and invite You in, or naked, and clothe You? 39 When did we see You sick, or in prison, and come to You?' 40 The King will answer and* *say to them, 'Truly I say to you, to the extent that you did it to one of these brothers of Mine, even the least of them, you did it to Me.'"*

Believers are the instruments of Christ to carry the gospel to the world and meet the needs of all people. He has given believers the power and gifts of the Spirit and word of God to meet the needs. Serving God and meeting the needs of others is a blessing to both.

Sometimes He may have to get your attention if you are rebellious. Don't be as hard headed as Paul when God wanted him in His family to carry out His will. Don't make serving God as difficult as it was for Saul who ended up on the ground with his face in the dirt before God got his attention.

Acts 9:3-6 *As he was traveling, it happened that he was approaching Damascus, and suddenly a light from heaven flashed around him; 4 and he fell to the ground and heard a voice* *saying to him, "Saul, Saul, why are you persecuting Me?" 5 And he said, "Who are You, Lord?" And He said, "I am Jesus whom you are persecuting, 6 but get up and enter the city, and it will be told you what you must do."*

Once he received his assignment from the Lord to be a missionary to the Gentiles he was faithful to his calling. It wasn't without hardships as we read in 2 Corinthians 11. He was successful in the ministry but he paid a price not many would or could endure.

The early church in Acts 17:6 states "These men (people of God) who have upset the world have come here also." The church was growing.

Their message of faith was built on the power of God and truth. The gospel was preached throughout the then known world. Many believed and churches began to flourish.

Romans 1:16-17 *For I am not ashamed*

of the gospel, for it is the power of God for salvation to everyone who believes, to the Jew first and also to the Greek. 17 For in it the righteousness of God is revealed from faith to faith; as it is written, "But the righteous man shall live by faith."

The cross does not discriminate against anyone. The gospel is for *whosoever will come and take of the water freely.* (Revelation 22:17d) (KJV) It is a symbol of God's love and an escape from His wrath.

Galatians 3:27-28 *For all of you who were baptized into Christ have clothed yourselves with Christ. 28 There is neither Jew nor Greek, there is neither slave nor free man, there is neither male nor female; for you are all one in Christ Jesus.*

In the flesh there is a difference but not according to the Spirit. We are brothers and sisters in the Lord.

We have been set free from our sin.

Revelation 1:5 ... *and from Jesus Christ, the faithful witness, the firstborn of the dead, and the ruler of the kings of the earth. To Him who loves us and released us from our sins by His blood ..."*

Life without Jesus is a life without water and food. Without His spiritual nutrition one will spiritually die and be separated from the Lord eternally.

The Samaritan woman at the well in John 4 is an example that pleases the Lord. It's a word picture of this woman receiving living water; drinking and thirsting no more.

John 4:10-11 *Jesus answered and said to her, "If you knew the gift of God, and who it is who says to you, 'Give Me a drink,' you would have asked Him, and He would have given you living water." 11 She said to Him, "Sir, You have nothing to draw with and the well is deep;*

where then do You get that living water?"

After a discussion about her husbands and the Messiah coming and about the Spirit, He declared to her in verse 26, "I who speak to you am He."

This illustration is a spiritual transformation of a woman and then becoming a witness for Jesus. A perfect example of how a believer can be a witness for Jesus and how faith can change a life.

When we choose to walk in faith it is an act of our will to a life with tremendous rewards. Faith is an action word which will reap benefits from the unseen in heavenly places.

I remember as a young adult I read the books *The Power of Positive Thinking,* by Norman Vincent Peale and *How to Win Friends and Influence People,* by Dale Carnegie. *The Power of Positive Thinking* had a good message with scripture but I wasn't a Christian at the time. These books helped inspire me to seek Him. Both books were good reads and interesting. It wasn't until I was born again and began reading the word by faith that the Holy Spirit provided the power to change my heart. Faith is the key to all God has to offer.

Hebrews 4:2 *For indeed we have had good news preached to us, just as they also; but the word they heard did not profit them, because it was not united by faith in those who heard.* (Those who sinned in the wilderness.)

Being born again was the beginning of my transformed life.

Proverbs 3:5-6 *Trust in the Lord with all your heart And do not lean on your own understanding. 6 In all your ways acknowledge Him, And He will make your paths straight.*

God is trying to teach us how to respond to and not react to the uncertainties of life. From my first encounter with Jesus, the Holy Spirit, His word and my spiritual mentors I began a journey that has been life changing. I spent many years under several mentors who knew the word better than anyone else I knew. They were a blessing to me. They taught me how to build my life on the rock instead of on sand. It was the best decision I ever made.

My hope and faith have grown through the years as I have studied the word. I have come to enjoy reading and studying God's word.

Don't reject or turn away from God as some do, the consequences are deadly. The scripture states we as people condemn ourselves because we choose to live by our own desires. Unless we repent and accept Christ, we will spend eternity without Jesus.

God is merciful, forgiving and full of grace. Amazing grace is available to all who repent and receive Jesus as Savior.

Ravi Zacharias, a wise Christian man of God stated, "A man rejects God neither because of intellectual demands nor because of the scarcity of evidence. A man rejects God because of a moral resistance that refuses to admit his need for God."

I have spoken about the tests of life and faith the last few pages. I wonder where we would be without God.

Hebrews 11:6 *And without faith it is impossible to please Him, for he who comes to God must believe that He is and that He is a rewarder of those who seek Him.*

Romans 10:17 *So faith comes from hearing, and hearing by the word of Christ.*

As we listen and hear the word our faith increases. As we read in James our faith should increase because of the tests we go through.

James 1:17 *Blessed is a man who perseveres under trial; for once he has been approved, he will receive the crown of life which the Lord has promised to those who love Him.*

Blessed means prosperity to our soul, inner state of joy and God's favor, hope, happiness and mercy.

Ephesians 1:3 *Blessed be the God and Father of our Lord Jesus Christ, who has blessed us with every spiritual blessing in the heavenly places in Christ …*

We read in Hebrews chapter three that God was not pleased with those who sinned in the wilderness.

Hebrews 3:17-18 *And with whom was He angry for forty years? Was it not with those who sinned, whose bodies fell in the wilderness? 18 And to whom did He swear that they would not enter His rest, but to those who were disobedient?*

Unbelief will separate us from God.

Disobedience diminishes faith. Don't neglect the word. Read and memorize the word to build your faith. You may find it helpful to write a scripture on a card to memorize.

Let me reiterate my question I asked at the beginning of this chapter. Is there not a cause? Yes, there is. And that is the function of the New Testament church; to build God's kingdom with those who truly believe in His work at the cross of Calvary through His son, Jesus Christ.

Luke 17:21 *"... for behold, the kingdom of God is in your midst."*

Acts 1:8 *"But you will receive power when the Holy Spirit has come upon you; and you shall be My witnesses both in Jerusalem, and in all Judea and Samaria, and even to the remotest part of the earth."*

Jesus has given us a mandate to go into our world and share His love, mercy, forgiveness and salvation. We know the early church served the local regions, Judea and parts of the uttermost regions of the then known world. Today we are the uttermost part of the world. There are still parts of the world that need to hear about Jesus. Most of these parts of the world are served by missionaries. Missionaries need financial support. We can read in the book of Acts and Paul's writing that missionaries were cared for and churches' needs were met. The kingdom is growing and there are many needs.

Ephesians 4:11-13 *And He gave some as apostles, and some as prophets, and some as evangelists, and some as pastors and teachers, 12 for the equipping of the saints for the work of service, to the building up of the body of Christ; 13 until we all attain to the unity of the faith, and of the knowledge of the Son of God, to a* *mature man, to the measure of the stature which belongs to the fullness of Christ …*

We read in these verses the saints are being equipped for ministry to build up the body of Christ. These verses were not only true in the early church but also in today's churches. Our pastors cannot be the only ones to minister in our communities. There are many needs to be met and they are to be met by the believers. The church can only be as effective as the congregation who serves. After all we have been prepared by God according to Ephesians 2:10, "We are His workmanship created for Good works." So as we grow in our personal knowledge and the grace of God we are to share our life and His word with others.

I could continue writing about this "Just Cause"; however, I think you get the idea. There are many more scriptures to support this theme. My prayer is these words of encouragement will prompt new growth in each of us and successful programs with Jesus being the chief cornerstone.

The important functions for a successful church are:

1. Prayer

Matthew 7:7 *"Ask, and it will be given to you; seek, and you will find; knock, and it will be opened to you."*

Acts 6:4 *"'But we will devote ourselves to prayer and to the ministry of the word.'"*

Prayer opens a channel of communication with God

2. Financial support

Malachi 3:10 *Bring the whole tithe into the storehouse, so that there may be food in My house, and test Me now in this," says the Lord of hosts, "if I will not open for you the windows* of heaven and pour out for you a blessing until it overflows.

2 Corinthians 8 & 9 speak of giving liberally and out of our abundance to those in need. God loves a cheerful giver.

3. Loving others

1 John 4:7-8 *Beloved, let us love one another, for love is from God; and everyone who loves is born of God and knows God. 8 The one who does not love does not know God, for God is love.*

God has and is equipping us for His goals, building relationships and changing lives.

At times we all fall short of these Christian standards because of distracting issues of life. Christians are not always perfect. We should confess our faults and continue to walk in the light. The closer you walk with Him the sooner you recognize your need for Him.

John 8:31-32 *So Jesus was saying to those Jews who had believed Him, "If you continue in My word, then you are truly disciples of Mine; 32 and you will know the truth, and the truth will make you free."*

Sometimes we may wonder, why am I NOT as free as I want to be. Notice in verse 31 He says, *If you continue in my word*, then we would be free and be overcomers. I would rather live after His prescription for life than the prescription the world offers. He will set us free from guilt, shame and sin.

Love Him because He first loved us and be worthy of our ambassadorship. After all, we now belong to Jesus and not ourselves.

Philippians 1:6 *For I am confident of this very thing, that He who began a good work in you will perfect it until the day of Christ Jesus.*

Embrace the Christian life and a <u>VIBRANT</u> Christian harvest.

Joshua 1:5B-6A *"... I will be with you; I will not fail you or forsake you. 6 Be strong and courageous ..."*

Thanks be to Jesus for the cross. The cross was a tree of death for Jesus, but a tree of life to believers. The tree in the garden brought spiritual death to humanity. Now a tree has brought life to humanity.

1 Peter 2:24 *He Himself bore our sins in His body on the cross, so that we might die to sin and live to righteousness; for by His wounds you were healed.*

Colossians 3:17 *Whatever you do in word or deed, do all in the name of the Lord Jesus, giving thanks through Him to God the Father.*

The God of all creation has your back. With God all things are possible. I remember in about the fourth grade my teacher told our class, "Can't never did anything". That is more scriptural than I thought. I will never forget that statement.

Philippians 4:13 *I can do all things through Him who strengthens me.*

A revelation of truth comes from the word and a personal relationship with God, NOT from how many degrees you have.

This country has seen many changes in the last few years - Covid, violence, food shortages, high prices, immigration problems, drought, floods, tornados, loss of jobs, closed schools, moral issues, and many other problems. I see so much suffering and tragedy people are experiencing worldwide and our freedoms are gradually slipping away. I believe God is awakening the church to shake the visible wordly culture, progressive and woke ideas in our government, our country and being taught in schools. It seems there is no right or wrong any more. There are wars and rumors of war all because of sin and evil in the hearts of man. There do not seem to be many answers other than the Lord's intervention. Man needs to turn to Jesus Christ. The church should be bold and spread the gospel in our communities, country and world. We should stand for moral and righteous conduct in our society. We need to trust our sovereign, loving and good God. One day there will be a new world order with Jesus as king over a new heaven and earth. Our future is in his hands.

Philippians 2:13 ... *for it is God who is at work in you, both to will and to work for His good pleasure.*

Philippians 2:15-16 ... *so that you will*

prove yourselves to be blameless and innocent, children of God above reproach in the midst of a crooked and perverse generation, among whom you appear as lights in the world, 16 holding fast the word of life, so that in the day of Christ I will have reason to glory because I did not run in vain nor toil in vain.

Sharing Your Faith

Many have asked me how I share my faith. The answer is I have been reading and studying the word and researching commentaries for many years. This is a help for me as I share my faith in Jesus and the love of God. I also share by telling people how Jesus has changed my life and tell them what he means to me.

I have been sharing my testimony, the benefits of faith and guiding people spiritually for many years. This has worked well for me. I am always willing at any time to talk to people about Jesus.

Recently one of the high school rodeo cowboys at a rodeo expressed some anxiety about his upcoming event. I shared Jesus and some scripture about anxiety with him. I told him to believe in the word, be confident in his ability, to fear not and cast his care on the Lord. He did and won his event that day.

These high school rodeos are held one weekend once a month in Lincoln, California. I share God's word Sunday morning at a church service. On Saturday and Sunday mornings before the rough stock events I share the word, a salvation message and pray a blessing over the riders before they ride. I encourage them, give them a word of confidence, tell them to love one another, enjoy their ride and live for the Lord.

There are usually fifteen to twenty teenage youth present and several fathers at this meeting behind the bucking chutes. It is a good time of fellowship and encouragement for these young cowboys.

In view of this chapter have you put your faith in action to benefit the body and lost souls in our community?

A couple of the last verses I am using to close this chapter are from Jesus Himself, who is seated at the right hand of the father in heaven.

Revelation 1:5-8 ... *and from Jesus Christ, the faithful witness, the firstborn of the dead, and the ruler of the kings of the earth. To Him who loves us and released us from our sins by His blood— 6 and He has made us to be a kingdom, priests to His God and Father—to Him be the glory and the dominion forever and ever. Amen. 7 BEHOLD, HE IS COMING WITH THE CLOUDS, and every eye will see Him, even those who pierced Him; and all the tribes of the earth will mourn over Him. So it is to be. Amen.*

8 "I am the Alpha and the Omega," says the Lord God, "who is and who was and who is to come, the Almighty."

Revelation 1:18 *"… and the living One; and I was dead, and behold, I am alive forevermore, and I have the keys of death and of Hades."*

Jesus is the one you want to know if you want to go to heaven.

If you have not accepted Christ after reading the first four chapters I would ask why you have not made a decision for Jesus? The answer to this question will determine your destiny and where you will spend eternity.

1 Thessalonians 5:21-24 *… but examine everything carefully; hold fast to that which is good; 22 abstain from every form of evil.*

23 Now may the God of peace Himself sanctify you entirely; and may your spirit and soul and body be preserved complete, without blame at the coming of our Lord Jesus Christ. 24 Faithful is He who calls you, and He also will bring it to pass.

2 Timothy 4:22 *The Lord be with your spirit. Grace be with you.*

6

FOXES IN OUR VINEYARD

Song of Solomon 2:14-16 *"O my dove, in the clefts of the rock, In the secret place of the steep pathway, Let me see your form, Let me hear your voice; For your voice is sweet, And your form is lovely."* 15 *"Catch the foxes for us, The little foxes* *that are ruining the vineyards, While our vineyards are in blossom. 16 My beloved is mine, and I am his; He pastures his flock among the lilies."*

These verses are mainly about a relationship in poetic language about King Solomon and his fiance. She is describing this beautiful relationship and how the little foxes can intrude into their lives by spoiling the vines and grapes. A fox can be a nuisance in this context by disrupting a relationship or a marriage. This is also a picture of Jesus and His bride. Both of these examples are describing a love affair with a disruption from the outside of a relationship.

These pesky foxes can interrupt a potential relationship and our walk with the Lord. They can be a real disadvantage to a marriage and our Christian life. These foxes represent worldliness to the Christian walk and the church. They can be described as false teachers, deceivers of the flock, people who cause divisions and disruption in the body of Christ.

We are responsible for stewardship and accountable to the born again life. So put your foot down for Jesus. Believers are the bride of Christ and one day they will be invited to the marriage supper of the Lamb. We should not be married to the world or allow a fox to permeate our lives and distract the body.

If you have ever sat straddling a fence or have had one foot in the world and one foot in the church, you know how uncomfortable that can be. It is difficult to live two different lives. Choose Jesus over the world. As James 1:5-8 says, *But if any of you lacks wisdom, let him ask of God, who gives to all generously and without reproach, and it will be given to him. 6 But he must ask in faith without any doubting, for the one who doubts is like the surf of the sea, driven and tossed by the wind. 7 For that man ought not to expect that he will receive anything from the Lord, 8 being a double-minded man, unstable in all his ways.*

Warning against the foxes:

1 Timothy 6:3-4 *If anyone advocates a different doctrine and does not agree with sound words, those of our Lord Jesus Christ, and with the doctrine conforming to godliness, 4he is conceited and understands nothing; but he has a morbid interest in controversial questions and disputes about words, out of which arise envy, strife, abusive language, evil suspicions ...*

How to get rid of the foxes:

James 4:7-8 *Submit therefore to God. Resist the devil and he will flee from you. 8 Draw near to God and He will draw near to you. Cleanse your hands, you sinners; and purify your hearts, you double-minded.*

2 Peter 3:17-18 *You therefore, beloved, knowing this beforehand, be on your guard so that you are not carried away by the error of unprincipled men and fall from your own* *steadfastness, 18 but grow in the grace and knowledge of our Lord and Savior Jesus Christ. To Him be the glory, both now and to the day of eternity. Amen.*

So we should humble ourselves before God and let the words of the Lord dwell in our hearts and minds.

Does anyone have any foxes lurking around in your life? These foxes can be a hindrance to living an overcoming life. I believe most of us have foxes in our relationships with each other, ourselves and with our Lord. However, if we confess our faults we can be forgiven and cleansed.

Overcoming the old nature can be a struggle for believers. None of us are perfect in our performance on a daily basis. Satan has a quiver full of fiery, wicked arrows to launch at Christians. We have an advantage over Satan if we put on the whole armor of God as instructed in Ephesians 6:10-18. We need God's full armor to withstand an attack and be overcomers. We need to renew our mind and thoughts to overcome the lust of the flesh, lust of the eyes and the pride of life. These lusts are not of the Father but of the world.

John writes in Revelation about Christians overcoming the accuser.

Revelation 12:11 *"And they overcame him because of the blood of the Lamb and because of the word of their testimony, and they did not love their life even when faced with death."*

I have used this verse when I felt oppressed by the accuser. My faith in God's word and in God lifted the oppression. Thank the Lord.

The Lord has equipped believers with the word to be Christian soldiers. He teaches us to use spiritual armor, the word and prayer with enabling power to be overcomers. Our battle is against the sinful nature and powers of darkness. It's casting down worldly wisdom and knowledge and applying God's knowledge and wisdom. Read Galatians 2:20 and Galatians 5:24-25.

Psalm 91:1-4 *He who dwells in the shelter of the Most High*
Will abide in the shadow of the Almighty.
2 I will say to the LORD, "My refuge and my fortress,
My God, in whom I trust!"
3 For it is He who delivers you from the snare of the trapper
And from the deadly pestilence.
4 He will cover you with His pinions,
And under His wings you may seek refuge;
His faithfulness is a shield and bulwark.

God provides protection and the enemy wants to trap you.

Do you believe there is a devil? Jesus did. He battled with him while He was in the wilderness for forty days. After being tempted His final statement to the devil was, "Worship the Lord your God and serve him only." Read Matthew 4:1-10.

The devil tries to corrupt, distort, disrupt, cause chaos and scheme against God's people, much like an adult fox. We have access to the power of God to make us victorious. Our faith should be strong, courageous and filled with hope.

God's Garden

When I was a young teenager my father always had a garden. It was well manicured - planting, fertilizing, tilling the ground, hoeing weeds, and cutting out the old to stimulate new growth. He sprayed for bugs to keep the enemies out of the garden. He planted all kinds of vegetables and melons. He worked to keep his garden productive and free of the weeds and bugs. He taught my brothers and me how to have a good work ethic. We worked with him daily in our garden and family orchard. We enjoyed the fruit of our labor.

Just as my father was determined to keep his garden productive and free of weeds and insects, we have a Heavenly Father that wants to protect us and help our spiritual garden be fruitful. God's plan is to groom believers and to fulfill His purpose in each one of us.

Psalm 92:12-15 *The righteous man will flourish like the palm tree,*

He will grow like a cedar in Lebanon.
13 Planted in the house of the LORD,
They will flourish in the courts of our God.
14 They will still yield fruit in old age;
They shall be full of sap and very green,
15 To declare that the LORD is upright;
He is my rock, and there is no unrighteousness in Him.

I like verse 14, *They will still yield fruit in old age* ...

Spiritual freedom comes when we are

faithful, responsible and obedient. Our spiritual life needs maintenance to be fruitful. When our new life is active and alive our old life diminishes.

Ezekiel 36:9 *"For, behold, I am for you, and I will turn to you, and you will be cultivated and sown."*

We should put down spiritual roots in the spiritual realm. We should feed and care for our new creation and be about God's work. This principle is found in the agricultural world. Plant a seed or a plant in the nurturing soil, let it grow with nourishment and produce fruit. Soil equates to our heart, water is Jesus, fertilizer is the Holy Spirit and weed control is the word of God. We will have a harvest of 30, 60 or 100 fold.

Mark 4:19 (Parable of the sower) *"… but the worries of the world, and the deceitfulness of riches, and the desires for other things enter in* *and choke the word, and it becomes unfruitful."*

There are three causes for failure: cares of this world, deceitfulness of riches and lusts of other things. So if you don't care for your spiritual garden you will not be fruitful. You should be willing to yield to the Holy Spirit as He cuts away the dead branches. As you abide in Jesus you will bear fruit and glorify the Father. He wants to reign in your heart.

John 15:5 *"I am the vine, you are the branches; he who abides in Me and I in him, he bears much fruit, for apart from Me you can do nothing."*

Wake up as the prodigal son did when he recognized the error of his ways and left the ashes of his life behind and began his new life filled with hope.

We have been called and set apart to be holy as God is holy. We have been warned to not harden our heart or fall away from the Lord. Don't allow your faith to diminish.

Isaiah 58:11 *And the LORD will continually guide you, And satisfy your desire in scorched places, And give strength to your bones; And you will be like a watered garden, And like a spring of water whose waters do not fail.*

When we are in the wilderness we need the Lord's refreshing grace.

Isaiah 61:3 … *to grant those who mourn in Zion,*

    giving them a garland instead of ashes,
    the oil of gladness instead of mourning,
    the mantle of praise instead of a spirit of fainting.
    so they will be called oaks of righteousness,
    the planting of the LORD, that He may be glorified.

What a breath of fresh air.

Isaiah 61:10-11 *I will rejoice greatly in the LORD,*

my soul will exult in my God;

for He has clothed me with garments of salvation,

He has wrapped me with a robe of righteousness,

as a bridegroom decks himself with a garland,

and as a bride adorns herself with her jewels.

11 For as the earth brings forth its sprouts,

and as a garden causes the things sown in it to spring up,

so the LORD God will cause righteousness and praise

to spring up before all the nations.

Are you tilling your ground with the word? What is sown brings forth life. Just as the Lord set Israel apart from the world of old He now has established the church of "whosoever will come" to be a witness to the world. This is you and me.

John 4:35 *"Do you not say, 'There are yet four months, and then comes the harvest'? Behold, I say to you, lift up your eyes and look on the fields, that they are white for harvest."*

There is a harvest ready and we the people must spread the gospel of Good News. Be a cheerleader for Jesus! Embrace Jesus and become salt and light for Christ! We believers have a calling to enter into the harvest that is ready.

John 4:37-38 *"For in this case the saying is true, 'One sows and another reaps.' 38 I sent you to reap that for which you have not labored; others have labored and you have entered into their labor."*

Are we willing to obey the master and go into the harvest? We have been chosen for a purpose: sow the seed and reap souls for God. Jesus has prepared the way because of His death on a wooden cross. His blood that was spilled will cover the sin of those who will accept His sacrifice. Jesus has graciously demonstrated His power by opening blind eyes and deaf ears and has performed many other miracles. At times He had many followers because there were many needs to be met.

As believers we are ambassadors for Christ. We have been commissioned by the King of Kings and Lord of Lords to go into all the world and preach the gospel to every creature. A good place to begin would be with our family and neighbors.

Mark 16:15 *And He said to them, "Go into all the world and preach the gospel to all creation."*

So many more words could be said about Jesus. His truth will be revealed in us as we grow in faith. It is exciting to be a part of the harvest the master has called us to.

Colossians 1:10-12 … *so that you will walk in a manner worthy of the Lord, to please Him in all respects, bearing fruit in every good work and increasing in the knowledge of God; 11 strengthened with all power, according to His glorious might, for the attaining of all steadfastness and patience; joyously 12 giving thanks to the Father, who has qualified us to share in the inheritance of the saints in light.*

The Sword

The sword we will be using for this journey of growth and service is the Bible. The Bible consists of sixty-six books written on three continents by forty writers. The Old Testament has thirty-nine books and the New Testament has twenty-seven books. It has a total of over 750,000 words and it took eleven hundred years to write. There are 1189 chapters and 31,102 verses. Jesus fulfilled over three hundred Old Testament prophecies written about Him in the Old Testament. I have read if you just took eight of these prophecies about Jesus and six hundred men with mathematical wisdom they would come up with this number: one in ten to the seventeenth power probability that Jesus is who the Bible says He is. That is a huge number. Many men who researched the scriptures hundreds of years ago and up until now have believed the Bible is God's word.

The world needs the truth of the Bible. Share God's truth It changes our perspective on the world. In Revelation 19 Jesus is going to return on a white horse and mete out justice. The armies of heaven will follow. He will have a sharp sword in his mouth. He will rule the world and on His vesture and thigh He will have written "King of Kings and Lord of Lords."

The following two verses are prophecies about Jesus:

Zechariah 12:10 *"I will pour out on the house of David and on the inhabitants of Jerusalem, the Spirit of grace and of supplication, so that they will look on Me whom they have pierced; and they will mourn for Him, as one mourns for an only son, and they will weep bitterly over Him like the bitter weeping over a firstborn."*

Zechariah 13:6 *"And one will say to him, 'What are these wounds between your arms?' Then he will say, 'Those with which I was wounded in the house of my friends.'"*

These are very enlightening verses. With all these men of wisdom and over three hundred Old Testament prophecies fulfilled, can you doubt the authenticity of the Bible and that Jesus is the son of God? No, unless you reject the God of the Bible. Don't allow the Bible to lay on a table and collect dust. It's of no value to anyone on a table. Jesus deserves our faith and trust for new life.

It's what is written on the inside of the Bible that makes a difference in one's life. If you haven't given your heart to the Lord, do it. A cowboy friend told me, "Give God the reins of your life." I did that over fifty years ago and it revolutionized my life. Read and memorize the word of God and be transformed.

Hebrews 4:15-16 *For we do not have a high priest who cannot sympathize with our weaknesses, but One who has been tempted in all things as we are, yet without sin. 16 Therefore let us draw near with confidence to the throne of grace, so that we may receive mercy and find grace to help in time of need.*

So get ready, your harvest is ready. His grace and mercy is always available in time of need.

7

GUIDE FOR LIVING

Colossians 3:15-17 *Let the peace of Christ rule in your hearts, to which indeed you were called in one body; and be thankful. 16 Let the word of Christ richly dwell within you, with all wisdom teaching and admonishing one another with psalms* *and hymns and spiritual songs, singing with thankfulness in your hearts to God. 17 Whatever you do in word or deed, do all in the name of the Lord Jesus, giving thanks through Him to God the Father.*

This chapter begins with a few more chosen scriptures and several books in the Bible for recommended reading. These books are easy reading and contain practical advice for Christian living. The gospel of John, Romans, 1 and 2 Corinthians and Galations through Titus. Read them at your convenience. This isn't to say all the books are NOT important, they are. The ones recommended are a good beginning.

The Bible is man's owner's manual for life. Some people have life coaches to guide them through life. However, Jesus will guide you step by step on a lighted path filled with heavenly wisdom. After all, who knows more about people than Jesus, our creator. Isaiah 9:6 states he is a

Wonderful Counselor, Mighty God, Everlasting Father and Prince of Peace. (NLT)

1. **Colossians 2:3** … *in whom are hidden all the treasures of wisdom and knowledge.*

2. **1 Corinthians 2:9-10** *But just as it is written, "Things which eye has not seen and ear has not heard, And which have not entered the heart of man, All that God has prepared for those who love Him." 10 For to us God revealed them through the Spirit; for the Spirit searches all things, even the depths of God.*

Let self go and replace it with the word. Give your heart to Jesus and put him first in your life.

3. **Ephesians 1:17-20** … *that the God of our Lord Jesus Christ, the Father of glory, may give to you a spirit of wisdom and of revelation in the knowledge of Him. 18 I pray that the eyes of your heart may be enlightened, so that you will know what is the hope of His calling, what are*

the riches of the glory of His inheritance in the saints, 19 and what is the surpassing greatness of His power toward us who believe. These are in accordance with the working of the strength of His might 20 which He brought about in Christ, when He raised Him from the dead and seated Him at His right hand in the heavenly places …

These are wonderful benefits from the Lord. If you are a Christian and not experiencing these riches, it is important to stop and take inventory of life and ask the question, why am I missing these riches in my life? Paul suggested we need to test ourselves to see if we are in the faith. Any doubts, take the test of 2 Corinthians 13:5-10 and Romans 8:16.

The corner I live on has a stop sign at a "T" intersection. The sign is red instructing drivers to stop. The word STOP is printed on the sign in white letters. To disobey this directive could result in injury or death. In my law enforcement career, I have seen both. The vehicle code has many instructions and warnings about driving behavior to prevent accidents.

God's word has many scriptures about how Christians should live. When we disobey there are consequences to our choices. Christians should obey the word so we may reap His glorious inheritance for His people.

2 Corinthians 4:6 *For God, who said, "Light shall shine out of darkness," is the One who has shone in our hearts to give the Light of the knowledge of the glory of God in the face of Christ.*

So let the light and knowledge of Jesus shine. If your light is weak make sure you are plugged into the source.

2 Corinthians 4:7 *But we have this treasure in earthen vessels, so that the surpassing greatness of the power will be of God and not from ourselves.*

What a treasure we have received.

2 Corinthians 10:3-5 *For though we walk in the flesh, we do not war according to the flesh, 4 for the weapons of our warfare are not of the flesh, but divinely powerful for the destruction of fortresses. 5 We are destroying speculations and every lofty thing raised up against the knowledge of God, and we are taking every thought captive to the obedience of Christ ...*

1 John 4:18-19 *There is no fear in love; but perfect love casts out fear, because fear involves punishment, and the one who fears is not perfected in love. 19 We love, because He first loved us.*

Remember fear can cripple us if we don't focus on God's love.

Romans 8:15 *"The Spirit you received does not make you slaves, so that you live in fear again; rather, the Spirit you received brought about your adoption to sonship. And by him we* *cry, "Abba, Father." (NIV)*

No more slavery to fear. No more slavery to the law. You are free from your past You now have a new life and are heirs to the riches of Heaven. Your "Abba Father" has made you a son and co-heir with his Son. Your Father rules the universe. Do you think He cares for you? Whatever your problems are in life, keep your eyes focused on the word and the Holy Spirit for wisdom. After all He has given us a life of power, love and a sound mind.

God has shown His love from Genesis to Revelation. In the beginning He created man to inhabit and care for His creation. This plan worked well until Adam and Eve sinned and had to be moved out of the garden.

As time went on, God chose Moses to deliver His people from Egypt. He gave Moses the Ten Commandments at Mount Sinai. This time was the beginning God would use to establish a relationship and moral code with the Jewish people and build a nation. The Ten Commandments were principles to live with God and their neighbors. He told the people He would show mercy to the people that love him if they would keep His commandments. He also told them they would prosper and all things would go well with them. So we read God's love is from which all blessings flow from the beginning to the end of time.

As history reads, the Jewish people were not always obedient to God's ways. Seems to me it was a love-hate relationship. Moving forward several thousand years into New Testament times, God sent His Son to establish a new covenant based on grace, mercy and love through the cross. His death, burial and resurrection purchased salvation for mankind. He demonstrated His love for mankind by filling our hearts with love by the Holy Spirit. We are now children of

God saved by grace through faith, not of works, it is the gift of God.

So the law was a teacher to draw us to Jesus who had the power to save and change our lives. The commandments did not have any power to change our wicked ways or save us from our sin. Satan wants to keep us uncomfortable and off balance in life. But God's plan for us is success. We can be overcomers as we appropriate God's armor that has been provided for believers.

Luke 10:27 *"You shall love the Lord your God with all your heart, and with all your soul, and with all your strength, and with all your mind; and your neighbor as yourself."*

We can potentially fulfill the law by loving God and one another. The law couldn't make anyone perfect, but we are now justified because of the blood of Jesus. We are declared perfect before the Father because of Jesus, however our performance (works) is not perfect. We should be thankful we have an advocate in Jesus. Amen.

2 Timothy 1:9 ... *who has saved us and called us with a holy calling, not according to our works, but according to His own purpose and grace which was granted us in Christ Jesus from all eternity* ...

John 8:12 *Then Jesus again spoke to them, saying, "I am the light of the world; he who follows Me will not walk in the darkness, but will have the Light of life."*

Even Isaiah 2:58 states to walk in the light of the Lord. Even though we are not perfect, God still has a purpose for us. We are salt and shining lights in the darkness to people in need of Jesus Christ.

2 Timothy 3:12 *Indeed, all who desire to live godly in Christ Jesus will be persecuted* ...

Persecution can bring anxiety and worry, but God has a solution.

Philippians 4:4-9 *Rejoice in the Lord always; again I will say, rejoice! 5 Let your gentle spirit be known to all men. The Lord is near. 6 Be anxious for nothing, but in everything by prayer and supplication with thanksgiving let your requests be made known to God. 7 And the peace of God, which surpasses all comprehension, will guard your hearts and your minds in Christ Jesus.*

8 Finally, brethren, whatever is true, whatever is honorable, whatever is right, whatever is pure, whatever is lovely, whatever is of good repute, if there is any excellence and if anything worthy of praise, dwell on these things. 9 The things you have learned and received and heard and seen in me, practice these things, and the God of peace will be with you.

Key thought: Worry is not an attribute of God. Don't waste your time with worry. Peace is an attribute of God. Peace will help with many ills of Christians. Don't be distracted by worry and be separated from God's peace. Worry is a human condition. I have read about ninety percent of what one worries about never happens. Prayer, praise, thanksgiving and worship equals the peace of God. Notice in Philippians 4:9 Paul told us, *Those things, which ye have both learned, and received, and heard, and seen in me, do: and the God of peace shall be with you.* (KJV) If you practice these things you will have God's peace. To benefit from these attributes, memorize and hide them in your heart.

John 14:27 *"Peace I leave with you; My peace I give to you; not as the world gives do I give to you. Do not let your heart be troubled, nor let it be fearful."*

Do you get it? Peace is offered from heaven!

Philippians 4:11-13 *Not that I speak*

from want, for I have learned to be content in whatever circumstances I am. 12 I know how to get along with humble means, and I also know how to live in prosperity; in any and every circumstance I have learned the secret of being filled and going hungry, both of having abundance and suffering need. 13 I can do all things through Him who strengthens me.

I find it interesting in two of these verses Paul said he had learned that his strength comes from Jesus.

Philippians 4:19-20 *And my God will supply all your needs according to His riches in glory in Christ Jesus. 20 Now to our God and Father be the glory forever and ever. Amen.*

God in Christ supplies our needs.

Romans 12:1-2 *Therefore I urge you, brethren, by the mercies of God, to present your bodies a living and holy sacrifice, acceptable to God, which is your spiritual service of worship. 2*

And do not be conformed to this world, but be transformed by the renewing of your mind, so that you may prove what the will of God is, that which is good and acceptable and perfect.

It doesn't matter about your past experiences. Jesus will renew your soul, heart and mind by the word. He will change your thoughts and change your life. So replace the ungodly things in your mind with the word of God. In order for the next two verses to be effective, you have to deny self and renew your thinking with the word.

Proverbs 4:23 *Watch over your heart with all diligence, For from it flow the springs of life.*

Proverbs 23:12 *Apply your heart to discipline and your ears to words of knowledge.*

Our heart and mind are influenced by what we put into them and it determines the path of life we walk. It is where the issues of life are born.

A man's heart determines the life we live. An unbeliever's heart is directed by the ways of the world. A believer's heart is to be directed by the word of God with enabling power from the Holy Spirit, or he/she will fall to the ways of the world.

The following verses give more information about the heart.

Hebrews 4:12-16 *For the word of God is living and active and sharper than any two-edged sword, and piercing as far as the division of soul and spirit, of both joints and marrow, and able to judge the thoughts and intentions of the heart. 13 And there is no creature hidden from His sight, but all things are open and laid bare to the eyes of Him with whom we have to do.*

14 Therefore, since we have a great high priest who has passed through the heavens, Jesus the Son of God, let us hold fast our confession. 15 For we do not have a high priest who cannot sympathize with our weaknesses, but One who has been tempted in all things as we are, yet without sin. 16 Therefore let us draw near with confidence to the throne of grace, so that we may receive mercy and find grace to help in time of need.

I understand these verses are numerous but read them with an open mind. Jesus knows all things about you. He was tested as we are but didn't sin and is now our high priest. Bring your problems to Him with confidence and allow his mercy and grace to minister to you. Jesus will do spiritual surgery on your heart with the word of God and give you a new heart.

God is in the process of building a personal relationship with His people. Jesus and the Father have a desire to help us with our life experiences. The Holy Spirit is our teacher and patiently guides us into this new life. The Spirit wants us to succeed and continually works in our life. We are to be humble coworkers with the Holy Spirit and open to his direction.

If you are a believer, do you have a divine calling to be used in the body? A divine call does not exempt us from trials or tests. So often we may discover ourselves falling back to the old way of resolving our daily problems and circumstances of life. It is not uncommon at times to find ourselves looking back for answers. There aren't usually any satisfactory answers in our past. Don't lock the Lord out of your decisions. He already has relief and answers of encouragement in His word. Look up and not back. Wrong thinking will not give you a good answer. Look to Jesus who has all knowledge and wisdom in the word of God.

He wants His thoughts and ways to become our ways. A time of searching and drawing close to Him with an open heart will reap benefits. The more knowledge one has about Him and His word the less fear and anxiety you will have from the tests of life. The Savior who knows everything about you has compassion and love for you. If you have fallen away for a time, ask for forgiveness, lean on Him and be faithful. Come home as the prodigal son and receive the blessings of heaven. He is waiting for you with open arms.

1 Peter 4:12 *Beloved, do not be surprised at the fiery ordeal among you, which comes upon you for your testing, as though some strange thing were happening to you ...*

As Christians we must realize we are in a spiritual battle. A believer must not open the door to the old sinful nature. We must ask the author of the fruit of the Spirit for guidance, strength and His help for victory. We must learn to trust the master in our spiritual tests. Rejoice and be blessed; give honor and glory to the Lord.

I am reminded of Paul's statement:

Colossians 3:2 *Set your mind on the things above, not on the things that are on earth.*

The choice is yours to make.

Henrietta Mears said, "One of God's specialties is to make somebodies out of nobodies." She understood man's weakness and God's power to change lives.

We must remember the Bible is as relevant today as the day it was written. It gives direction to a meaningful life and a deeper relationship with God. It contains transforming power and truth from the Holy Spirit. He gives wisdom to engage in the spiritual warfare we face with the principalities and powers of darkness. We are spiritual people who need spiritual guidance.

Hebrews 12:2 *We do this by keeping our eyes on Jesus, the champion who initiates and perfects our faith. Because of the joy awaiting him, he endured the cross, disregarding its shame.*

Now he is seated in the place of honor beside God's throne. (NLT)

Notice the word states to keep "our eyes on Jesus." If we do, we won't faint or grow weary in doing good.

Ephesians 3:20 *Now to Him who is able to do far more abundantly beyond all that we ask or think, according to the power that works within us …*

To live the overcoming life, we need faith and the power of God. Our love for God should be growing and we need to be rooted and grounded in His word. If your faith is weak, ask God to help your unbelief. Remember the story of the man with the demonic son in Mark 9:22-24. Jesus spoke to him about his faith. The man said "I believe; help thou mine unbelief." (KJV) Don't hesitate to ask God to strengthen your faith. He rewards those that seek after Him.

The word of God was breathed from heaven. If we believe in heaven, we must believe and live by the written word.

2 Timothy 3:16-17 *All Scripture is inspired by God and profitable for teaching, for reproof, for correction, for training in righteousness; 17 so that the man of God may be adequate, equipped for every good work.*

Being a cowboy for many years I ensure my fences around the fields where the cattle spend the winter are secure. The cattle I care for have the assurance their feed, water, minerals and safety are provided. The fence provides for their safety and keeps them from straying from their fields. Several times a year I ride the fence line to maintain the integrity of the fence and to determine if any cattle are missing. The fence represents the word of God which keeps believers from straying off the narrow path and also provides for our spiritual welfare.

The word guides us in righteousness and equips us for the work of the Lord. I have learned as the word was breathed into the writers of the Bible I must breathe the word into my soul. It is only then that I can share the word with others. Take in the word and speak it out. It is life changing and will change lives.

Titus 1:9 … *holding fast the faithful word which is in accordance with the teaching, so that he will be able both to exhort in sound doctrine and to refute those who contradict.*

Blessings shall follow the Christian life if we walk in the Spirit and truth of His word.

The following from Solomon, writer of Ecclesiastes, concludes this chapter. He wrote that the worldly life is foolishness and the Godly life is rewarding. He closes with:

Ecclesiastes 12:13 *The conclusion, when*

all has been heard, is: fear God and keep His commandments, because this applies to every person.

"Fear God" for the believer means to be in awe of the majesty and glory of God, to be obedient and faithful to the ways of God. It is life, hope, wisdom and knowledge of God.

Solomon, the richest and smartest man that ever lived, has drawn the conclusion that God's way is the only way. God gave him his wisdom. Maybe we should follow his advice.

8
HOPE

Romans 15:4 *For whatever was written in earlier times was written for our instruction, so that through perseverance and the encouragement of the Scriptures we might have hope.*

Several years ago I heard or read a definition of hope from an unknown source. "Two robins sitting on a tree branch began to sing before dawn while waiting for the SUN to shine." That's a reasonably good definition of hope. A person who has faith in God has hope. If we walk in the light of the SON, He shines on us and cleanses us from all sin. When one believes in the gospel he has hope.

Titus 1:1-2 *Paul, a bond-servant of God and an apostle of Jesus Christ, for the faith of those chosen of God and the knowledge of the truth which is according to godliness, 2 in the hope of eternal life, which God, who cannot lie, promised long ages ago ...*

Our confidence and hope grows and encourages us to be overcomers. As we trust and believe in God that He will be faithful we can believe our purpose will be fulfilled in Him. Jesus' message of hope is salvation. I am thankful for His transforming grace.

2 Corinthians 3:18 *But we all, with*

unveiled face, beholding as in a mirror the glory of the Lord, are being transformed into the same image from glory to glory, just as from the Lord, the Spirit.

Romans 15:13 *Now may the God of hope fill you with all joy and peace in believing, so that you will abound in hope by the power of the Holy Spirit.*

Romans 8:35 *Who will separate us from the love of Christ? Will tribulation, or distress, or persecution, or famine, or nakedness, or peril, or sword?*

So if you read the end of Romans 8 you will discover nothing, nothing can separate us from God's love and hope.

Romans 5:5 ... *and hope does not disappoint, because the love of God has been poured out within our hearts through the Holy Spirit who was given to us.*

Read a story of faith and hope in Acts 27:14-44 and Acts 28:1-11. If you read these verses notice verses 20, 25, 31 and 44. We read Paul is enroute to Rome by sea to stand before Caesar. A large group was on the ship with Paul. They began their voyage and because of storms made several stops. They began their journey again against Paul's advice but the captain wanted to proceed. He was concerned about the potential storms that might arise and they wouldn't complete their trip.

After they set sail a violent wind came up and the ship and lives were in danger. Neither sun nor stars appeared for many days. They went without food during that time. The people on board lost all hope of surviving. Many of the men were anxious, afraid and scared believing they would die. Paul urged them to keep up their courage and none would be lost except the ship. Paul told them an angel of the Lord spoke to him and told him he must stand before Caesar. However, they

Hope

must stay in the ship to remain safe. With many struggles all arrived on the island of Malta after the ship had broken up because of the storm. Many swam and others used planks to float to shore.

They were wet and cold and a fire was built by the natives. Paul was bitten by a viper from the wood he was placing on the fire. The natives believed he would die but he didn't so they thought he was a god.

The father of Publius was sick. Paul prayed and laid hands on him and he was healed. Many people on the island had diseases and came to Paul and he healed them.

Eventually they left Malta and arrived in Rome.

We read in Daniel 3:12-29 about three Jewish men Shadrach, Meshach and Abed-nego. They refused to worship an image made by King Nebuchadnezzar. He told them if they didn't worship the image they would be cast into a fiery furnace. They said God was able to deliver them and if not they would not worship the golden image. They refused, were bound and were cast into the fiery furnace. The king looked into the furnace and saw a fourth person "like the Son of God" (KJV) and none of them were hurt. When they came out, none of them were affected by the fire. Nebuchadnezzar was amazed and said, *Blessed be the God of Shadrach, Meshach and Abed-nego, who has sent His angel and delivered His servants.*

These three young men had hope and an expectation that God would deliver them from the fire and out of the hand of the king. They had faith and hope of deliverance. We see a picture of the Son of God in the midst of the fire. In the miracles of God He is present.

Isaiah 43:1-2 *But now thus saith the LORD that created thee, O Jacob, and he that formed thee, O Israel, Fear not: for I have redeemed thee, I have called thee by thy name;*

thou art mine. 2 When thou passest through the waters, I will be with thee; and through the rivers, they shall not overflow thee: when thou walkest through the fire, thou shalt not be burned; neither shall the flame kindle upon thee. (KJV)

Isaiah 43:4-5a *Since thou wast precious in my sight, thou hast been honourable, and I have loved thee: therefore will I give men for thee, and people for thy life. 5 Fear not: for I am with thee* … (KJV)

These verses are speaking of Jacob; however, God loves His people and He is present with us.

When we know God or hear a word from Him and are obedient as were Paul, Shadrach, Meshach and Abed-nego, our hope will be realized. When a person experiences an event of this magnitude, they will need this kind of faith and hope.

Psalm 31:24 *Be strong and let your heart take courage, all you who hope in the Lord!*

In the Old Testament many times we find hope. Even when His people were disobedient there was always the message of repentance. If His people would be obedient and turn back to Him, He would grant them favor.

Isaiah 1:18 *Come now, and let us reason together, says the Lord, though your sins are as scarlet, they will be as white as snow; though they are red like crimson, they will be like wool.'"*

Ezekiel 36:25-26 *"Then I will sprinkle clean water on you, and you will be clean; I will cleanse you from all your filthiness and from all your idols. 26 Moreover, I will give you a new heart and put a new spirit within you; and I will remove the heart of stone from your flesh and give you a heart of flesh."*

This Old Testament scripture states there is an opportunity for hope and salvation through the cross of Jesus

Christ.

Isaiah 53:5-6 *But He was pierced through for our transgressions, He was crushed for our iniquities; The chastening for our well-being fell upon Him, and by His scourging we are healed. 6 All of us like sheep have gone astray, each of us has turned to his own way; But the Lord has caused the iniquity of us all to fall on Him.*

Isaiah 53:10 *But the Lord was pleased to crush Him, putting Him to grief; If He would render Himself as a guilt offering, He will see His offspring, He will prolong His days, and the good pleasure of the Lord will prosper in His hand.*

Isaiah 53 was one of the greatest prophecies of hope for mankind. It is a prophecy about the coming Messiah, Jesus, who died for our sins and was raised from the dead. Hallelujah and praise the Lord. This prophecy is a positive message of hope; one that should build people up. After all, it is a message of new life and it has been fulfilled for over two thousand years. Because of the cross we can have a life of forgiveness.

Thanks be to Jesus for His life from the cradle to His resurrection.

The following are more scriptures on hope.

Hebrews 6:18-20 ... *so that by two unchangeable things in which it is impossible for God to lie, we who have taken refuge would have strong encouragement to take hold of the hope set before us. 19 This hope we have as an anchor of the soul, a hope both sure and steadfast and one which enters within the veil, 20 where Jesus has entered as a forerunner for us, having become a high priest forever according to the order of Melchizedek.*

This promise is from a God who cannot lie with a message of hope and entrance into the Holy of Holies.

Colossians 1:27 *To whom God willed to make known what is the riches of the glory of this mystery among the Gentiles, which is Christ in you, the hope of glory.*

A mystery for ages now unveiled.

Colossians 1:5 … *because of the hope laid up for you in heaven, of which you previously heard in the word of truth, the gospel* …

Faith in the gospel secures eternal life for believers.

Titus 2:13 … *looking for the blessed hope and the appearing of the glory of our great God and Savior, Christ Jesus* …

The hope of all believers.

2 Timothy 4:8 *In the future there is laid up for me the crown of righteousness, which the Lord, the righteous Judge, will award to me on that day; and not only to me, but also to all who* *have loved His appearing.*

A crown of righteousness to those who love His appearing. This verse is the fulfillment of our hope.

In his book, *A Cowboy's Faith*, by cowboy author Jack Terry, June 1, 2001, Harvest House Publishers edition, he wrote, "It is the steadfastness of hope that allows us to endure."

Without hope no one has much of a reason for living.

1 Peter 1:3 *Blessed be the God and Father of our Lord Jesus Christ, who according to His great mercy has caused us to be born again to a living hope through the resurrection of Jesus Christ from the dead ...*

Now that is something to hold close to your heart.

The following is a personal note about hope and peace that I am sharing to give Jesus the glory. My prescription for peace was and is Jesus. Hope is necessary for a meaningful life.

Over thirty years ago I had an unsuspected crisis in my life. (A crisis can be any event that turns your life upside down.) I was caught completely off guard. I was driven to my knees several hours every evening for a month. After I came home from work each evening I would have dinner and watch the evening news. I would then begin my spiritual battle. For about two hours I would read the word, pray, worship and sometimes cry. (It is okay for guys to cry.) I sang Christian choruses. I didn't sing well any time but God was gracious to listen. I would also read the word during the day when time allowed.

I had many concerns on my mind which I knew would change and affect my life. My daily life and commitments continued because of my obligations. However, I was experiencing mild symptoms of stress. This stress took away most desires to do any more than the things for which I was responsible. (If stress or any spiritual or physical problem becomes unbearable don't hesitate to seek counseling.) I had five helpful sessions with a Christian counselor.

There were times I drove around town and the countryside to places I used to enjoy spending time with my friends from my past. I was looking for something I could grasp from the past, an acquaintance or old friend for companionship; wanting peace, hope and fellowship from humanity. The old memories I was looking for weren't there anymore, only in my mind.

I have disclosed this part of my life to share God's goodness and faithfulness. During this time, I was in need of a closer relationship with God. I was seeking comfort, peace and hope. My attention was now directed to the word, prayer and worship. I had to recharge myself each day by seeking God. God became my best friend. My new daily time with God brought me what I needed. My daily scripture reading was instrumental in my receiving spiritual strength and comfort. After several months of dedication and committing my future to God, life was looking much better. My hope and joy returned and I felt I could face any situation the enemy placed in my life, like David facing Goliath. My faith had increased. God has been very gracious to me. God was very instrumental in my recovery and I have been blessed. The last thirty years my life has changed with a different direction and purpose in life.

Now I can go to these same old locations which have new establishments and visit with my old friends. We enjoy the old memories and make new memories. We meet at a local restaurant every few months for a great two hours enjoying lunch together while talking about our retirement, health, children, grandkids and their events and sharing our current dreams. We talk about our high school and college days, old girlfriends, past employment, the cars we drove, beloved deceased buddies and the good old days of the sixties. Most of us drag raced on the street and in organized racing. It isn't long before our conversation drifts to fast cars and who won the races. Most of us drove Chevys, Fords, Pontiacs, Dodges or Plymouths. My last car I raced was a new 1966 Pontiac GTO. Most of the establishments we frequented in those days were the Yuba City Bowling Alley, A & W Drive In on Shasta Street in Yuba City, Shakey's Pizza on 12th Street in Marysville, the Frostie on Colusa Avenue and of course the Yuba City drive-in movies. Occasionally we left the Yuba-Sutter area and drove to Colusa, Chico and Sacramento. The cruise was a large part of the night out. The cruise was the main streets we traveled on the weekends in Yuba City and Marysville. Old memories are alive and well when we meet for lunch. (I even get nostalgic writing these memories down from my past.)

God's word and promises are true!

Lamentations 3:22-26 *The LORD's loving kindnesses indeed never cease, for His compassions never fail. 23 They are new every morning; Great is Your faithfulness. 24 "The LORD is my portion," says my soul, "therefore I have hope in Him." 25 The LORD is good to those who wait for Him, to the person who seeks Him. 26 It is good that he waits silently for the salvation of the LORD.*

Our inner man must be fed every day to remain spiritually strong. Our soul and heart are fed by renewing our mind with the word. My path to success and full recovery from my crisis is found in God's presence. You will learn more about His word, worship, prayers and maybe even improve your singing. Give God a chance to be a part of your crisis and tests in life. He will give you encouragement, comfort, strength and hope. It is worth more than money when God is on your side.

People need hope. I personally know how important hope is to everyone. It is where the rubber meets the road. It's like having a bad dream. You are in the ocean struggling to stay afloat and someone throws you a life jacket but it's always out of reach. You continue to flounder, beating the waves with no hope. Then you wake up and realize it was only a dream.

I remember reading some time ago about the German war camps. The writer said something to the effect that those who survived were the ones who were helping others and had hope.

Psalm 86:10-13 *For You are great and do wondrous deeds; You alone are God. 11 Teach me Your way, O Lord; I will walk in Your truth; Unite my heart to fear Your name. 12 I will give thanks to You, O Lord my God, with all my heart, And will glorify Your name forever. 13 For Your lovingkindness toward me is great, And*

You have delivered my soul from the depths of Sheol.

My daughter gave me this copy of the *Cowboy 10 Commandments*. I thought I would share them with you.

COWBOY 10 COMMANDMENTS

1. Just one God.
2. Honor yer Ma & Pa.
3. No letting tales or gossipin'.
4. Git yourself to Sunday meeting.
5. Put nothin' before God
6. No foolin' around with another fellow's gal.
7. No killin'.
8. Watch your mouth
9. Don't take what ain't yers.
10. Don't be hankerin' for yer buddy's stuff.

EPILOGUE

Looking back on my life of eighty years I can see how God has molded and made me who I am today. He has shown me his faithfulness, goodness, mercy, love, kindness and has blessed my life abundantly. From a humble beginning born and living in a small home in a farm labor camp spending my days in a thirty-five-pound peach lug box to living with my wife in our nice comfortable home we purchased on two acres with a horse barn, pasture and exercise arena for our horses and working cattle dogs. God has been good to me and He has given me the fulfillment of the life I desired. He has blessed me with my wife, three grown children, their families and six wonderful grandchildren who are all serving the Lord. I am so thankful for God's grace and blessings.

As a cowboy most of my life I have seen how the livestock protect each other and especially their babies from their enemies. On several occasions I have seen the cows I care for protecting their babies or young calves from dogs or coyotes. Wolves, foxes and other wild animals are a threat to livestock also. These predators have a scheme or plan to catch and kill vulnerable cattle and calves. I have witnessed four to five coyotes attempting to separate a mother cow from its calf by isolating the calf. The predators resemble a police swat team deploying officers in different locations to capture a suspect. When a cow sees her calf in trouble , she will bellow (a distress call) and all the other cows will respond and run to help scatter and drive off the dogs or coyotes. This is God's way of helping protect older or sick cows and helping livestock protect their young.

Cows need a cowboy and sheep need a shepherd. The role of the cowboy and shepherd is to protect, provide, minister care and keep their herd or flock in a secure environment. Many times day or night I have been called out to put cattle back into their fenced in pastures. A shepherd's rod and staff help the shepherd protect the sheep.

People are in need of a shepherd. Psalm 100 says we are His sheep. In John 10, Jesus says he is the good shepherd and lays down His life for His sheep. He tells us the thief (Satan) comes to steal, kill and destroy but He (Jesus) comes to give us life. The enemies of our livestock have the same goal as Satan. Both go about seeking who they can devour. People and livestock need guidance and protection in life. The Bible provides guidance and protection for His human sheep.

I was involved in helping with junior

and high school rodeo rough stock events of bucking horses and bull riding for many years. This led me to being involved in the production of junior bull riding events which included mutton busting, calf riding, steer riding and bull riding. These are dangerous events. I have worked with and prayed with these kids. These participants were taught the art of riding and wore safety and protective gear when riding. In the arena the riders have cowboy life savers known as bullfighters. There are usually two to three bullfighters in the arena and their job is to protect and save riders from the bucking bulls. When the rider is bucked off the bullfighters will step in front of the bull and direct it in a different direction to allow the rider to escape. Sometimes these bullfighters get tossed six feet in the air or get kicked while performing their duties. These riders and bullfighters develop a close relationship. Many of these riders have another life saver, Jesus Christ, who they put their trust and confidence in as Lord and Savior.

I have been a rodeo rough stock announcer many times over the past twenty years. An announcer tells the audience about the contestants, name of the livestock to be ridden (yes they have names), names of the people working in and around the arena, promote the rodeo sponsors, goodwill in the community and animal welfare. They open with prayer and promote patriotism; honoring the American Flag.

Times have changed in the last eighty years. Some for the good and some not so good. From the days of small town living where communication was a radio or television with three channels and rabbit ears with tin foil on them for better reception, personal mail, a party line telephone system and a small comfortable home when people would sit in the yard or on the porch and visit with each other while drinking their favorite beverage.

Most of our yards were open and welcoming, not surrounded by a six-foot fence as many are today.

People don't visit with each other like we did when I grew up. I miss the get togethers and games we played, good food and homemade ice cream. Family times were a time to socialize, get to know each other well and provide guidance for living. We spoke to each other face to face and did not text each other while in the same room. Family and friends were always welcome. If it was dinner time, mom would throw in extra potatoes, bread and dessert to provide for all.

Sadly, times such as these are mostly past. The world and technology has changed so much in the last twenty-five to thirty years. The internet and the World Wide Web became available to the general public and the smartphone with web browsing capabilities and millions of apps was introduced. Now with a $800 cell phone one has access to everything you want to know and you don't want to know. You can even lock yourself in your bedroom and get a college education. I am amazed at these modern times in which we live. I am still behind the times.

In 1999, my last years as a detective sergeant I experienced teenagers and young adults losing respect for authority. This lack of respect has now turned into rampant violence and destruction of life and property. Our worldly culture is now so opposed to God's wisdom and truth. In some cities our neighborhoods are decaying. The no lock door policy of most in my day and the neighborhood gatherings have diminished. Now we stay in locked homes inside fenced yards with security cameras, outdoor lights and security patrols.

Controversial and negative social media has affected society. An increasing amount of people are addicted to drugs and porn. Depression, loneliness, fear, sexual, emotional and physical abuse are on the rise. Other mental and physical issues are climbing. We need to get back to being a community of people and not rely on social media for pleasure. We need a change in direction and lifestyle. All of us have a heart (our innermost being).

The Bible teaches our hearts can be good or bad. Our thinking and thoughts determine the path we walk in life. Scripture says as a man thinks in his heart so he is and from the heart flows the issues of life. Romans 12:2 reminds us not to be conformed to the culture of this world but be transformed by the renewing of our mind with God's word. We need a change of heart and to get rid of some of our idols. An idol is anything that takes the place of God and causes our spiritual hearing to become dull. Our country needs a revival.

Our world is sitting on a teetering edge. Maybe some of you feel like you are sitting on a precarious edge. If any are experiencing loneliness, unhappiness, anxiety, fear or lack of peace, Jesus has the answer. He will help restore you.

If the sheep need shepherds and cattle need cowboys to provide for them, surely people need a heavenly shepherd to direct and provide for the people He created and loves. He has ascended to heaven to create a heavenly home for us.

I often think about our children and grandchildren and the future they face. I wonder what challenges they will face and what life will be like in another thirty years. Signs of the end times are much closer today than when I was a child.

Don't lose your joy. Look to Jesus the author and finisher of your faith. He is our refuge, comforter, encourager and strength. Invest your time in His word. His free gift of salvation is our hope of eternal life.

May your faith and hope stay strong. God is your refuge, strength and help in times of trouble. May God bless you and guide you on the trails you ride.

Galatians 1:3-4 *Grace to you and peace from God our Father and the Lord Jesus Christ, who gave Himself for our sins so that He might rescue us from this present evil age, according to the will of our God and Father ...*

CONTACT

If you would like to connect with Jim, you can reach him at this email: cowboyjimdurbin@gmail.com.

Made in the USA
Columbia, SC
29 November 2023